SUPPLEMENT TO
THE BOOK OF
Hymns

SUPPLEMENTAL WORSHIP RESOURCES 11

The United Methodist Publishing House
Nashville, Tennessee

SUPPLEMENT TO THE BOOK OF HYMNS

Copyright © 1982 The United Methodist Publishing House

ISBN 0-687-03757-3

ISBN 0-687-03758-1 (Accompanist's Edition)

MANUFACTURED BY THE PARTHENON PRESS AT
NASHVILLE, TENNESSEE, UNITED STATES OF AMERICA

Preface

The Supplement to the Book of Hymns is a collection of alternative congregational song selected from that which has been used in The United Methodist Church and the wider Christian community since the canon of *The Book of Hymns* was closed in 1963. This collection of alternative hymnody and psalmody includes selections from the Evangelical United Brethren Church; the old and new gospel hymn traditions; that identified as representative song by task forces from four ethnic minority groups within United Methodism, i.e., Native American, Afro-American, Hispanic, and Asian-American; and recent "standard" and "pop" hymnody.

In its editorial work, which spanned three years, the *Supplement* task force received from the general church and reviewed approximately fifteen hundred texts, some already with appropriate music settings.

In addition, the task force has been sensitive to the importance that United Methodists place on inclusive, nonsexist, and nondiscriminatory language. Accordingly, some word changes have been made in texts from the public domain. In the instances of copyrighted texts, every effort has been made to secure permission in order to make the appropriate changes.

An important feature of the *Supplement* is the "performance note," which appears at the top of the page and provides the music/liturgy leader suggestions as to how that particular selection might be used in musical, educational, and liturgical settings. Suggested introductions are indicated between brackets.

Deep appreciation is expressed to Gwen Pullen and Charles O. McNish of The United Methodist Publishing House for their careful attention to manuscript preparation and the printing of the *Supplement*; to Darrell Woomer for providing the scripture references; James A. Rogers, for providing the general index; Roger N. Deschner for providing the topical index; and to Joyce Ogden for assistance in cover design.

The *Supplement* task force consists of Jane Marshall (chairperson), Sara Collins, and James A. Rogers (secretary). The editor is Carlton R. Young. Consultants are Roger N. Deschner, Ellen Jane Lorenz Porter, and John Erickson.

The Section on Worship of the Board of Discipleship is the sponsor of the *Supplement,* which is the eleventh publication in its Supplemental Worship Resources (SWR) series. The Section on Worship did the basic planning, elected the editor and task force who have prepared the *Supplement,* and has given editorial oversight to this particular project that was requested by action of the 1976 General Conference.

Members of the Section on Worship (1976–80) included Louise H. Shown (chairperson), James F. White (chairperson, editorial committee), Paul F. Abel, Phyllis Close, Edward L. Duncan, Judy Gilreath, Bishop Robert E. Goodrich, Kay Hereford, Judith Kelsey-Powell, Marilyn Mabee, L. Doyle Masters*, William B. McClain, Carlton R. Young, Philip E. Baker, and Janet Lee (ex officio). Section on Worship staff included Melvin G. Talbert, Roberto Escamilla, Hoyt L. Hickman, Richard L. Eslinger, and Elise Shoemaker. Leaders of ethnic consultant groups were I-to Loh, Jefferson Cleveland, Lindy Waters*, and Rachel Achon.

*Deceased

All That Christians Have in Life

This creedal statement can be used as a litany, with one group singing the first 2½ lines and another echoing with the last two measures.

In a gentle two

1. All that Chris-tians have in life is a sto-ry and a song,
2. All that Chris-tians are in life: they are peo-ple of "the way,"
3. All that Chris-tians have and are is a pic-ture of their Lord,

bread and wine, a lit-tle faith and a long–ing to be-long;
led by hunch-es, lured by hope, now ex-cit-ed, then a-fraid;
is a sig-nal and a glimpse, is a ges-ture and a word;

1. 2.
that is what they have. That is what they have.
that is what they are. That is what they are.
that is where they are. That is where they

3.
are.

WORDS: Fred Kaan, 1975
MUSIC: Carlton Young, 1980

CREDO
77.77.55.

855
Alabaré (I Will Praise My Lord)

Refrain

* A-la-ba-ré, a-la-ba-ré, a-la-ba-ré a mi Se-ñor.

A-la-ba-ré, a-la-ba-ré, a-la-ba-ré a mi Se-ñor. *Fine*

Stanzas

1. Juan vi-ó el nú-mer-o, de los red-i-mi-dos, y
1. John saw the num-ber of all those re-deemed, and

to-dos a-la-ba-ban al Se-ñor. U-nos o-ra-ban,
all were sing-ing prais-es to the Lord. Thou-sands were pray-ing, ten

o-tros can-ta-ban, y to-dos a-la-ba-ban al Se-ñor. *to refrain*
thou-sands re-joic-ing, and all were sing-ing prais-es to the Lord.

** 2. No hay Dios tan gran-de co-mo Tu, No lo hay, no lo
** 2. There is no God as great as you, O Lord, there is none, there is

* Alabaré a mi Señor = "I will praise my Lord."

** The second stanza is commonly sung as a separate hymn, without a refrain, in Latin-American countries.

WORDS and MUSIC: Anonymous ; vs. 1, Revelation 5:11-14; 6:9-12; 19:6-8;   ALABARÉ
vs. 2, Matthew 17:20-21   Irregular with Refrain

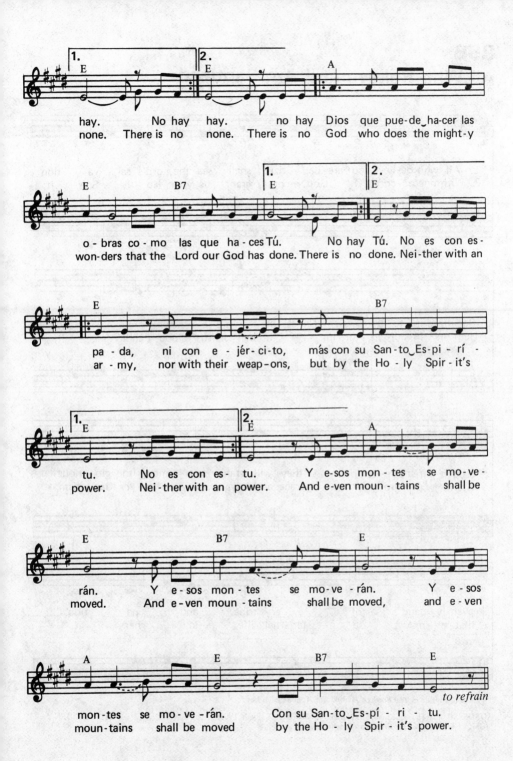

1. hay. No hay
none. There is no

2. hay. no hay Dios que pue-de ha-cer las
none. There is no God who does the might-y

o - bras co - mo las que ha - ces Tú.
won - ders that the Lord our God has done.

1. No hay Tú. No es con es -
There is no done. Nei - ther with an

pa - da, ni con e - jér - ci - to, más con su San - to Es - pi - rí -
ar - my, nor with their weap - ons, but by the Ho - ly Spir - it's

1. tu. No es con es -
power. Nei - ther with an

2. tu. Y e-sos mon - tes se mo - ve -
power. And e - ven moun - tains shall be

rán. Y e - sos mon - tes se mo - ve - rán. Y e - sos
moved. And e - ven moun - tains shall be moved, and e - ven

mon - tes se mo - ve - rán. Con su San - to Es - pí - ri - tu.
moun - tains shall be moved by the Ho - ly Spir - it's power.

to refrain

856
All Who Believe and Are Baptized

Unison

1. All who be-lieve and are bap-tized shall see the Lord's sal-va-tion;
2. With one ac-cord, O God, we pray, grant us your Ho-ly Spir-it;

Bap-tized in-to the death of Christ, they are a new cre-a-tion;
Help us in our in-fir-mi-ty through Je-sus' blood and mer-it;

Through Christ's re-demp-tion they will stand a-mong the glo-rious
Grant us to grow in grace each day by ho-ly Bap-tism,

heaven-ly band of ev-ery tribe and na-tion.
that we may e-ter-nal life in-her-it.

* This tune appears in *The Book of Hymns*, No. 4, in a higher key.

WORDS: Thomas Hansen Kingo, 1699; trans. by George A. T. Rygh, 1909
MUSIC: *Kirchengesänge*, Bohemian Brethren, 1566

'MIT FREUDEN ZART
87.87. 887.

All Who Love and Serve Your City

Unison, with strength

1. All who love and serve your cit-y, all who
2. In your day of loss and sor-row, in your
3. In your day of wealth and plen-ty, wast-ed
4. For all days are days of judg-ment, and the
5. Ris-en Lord, shall yet the cit-y be the

bear its dai-ly stress, All who cry for peace and
day of help-less strife, Hon-or, peace, and love re-
work and wast-ed play, Call to mind the word of
Lord is wait-ing still, Draw-ing near to all who
cit-y of de-spair? Come to-day, our Judge, our

jus-tice, all who curse and all who bless:
treat-ing, seek the Lord, who is your life.
Je-sus, "Work ye yet while it is day."
spurn him, of-fering peace from Cal-vary's hill.
Glo-ry, be its name, "The Lord is there!"

WORDS: Erik Routley, 1967; Luke 19:41; Ezekiel 48:35
MUSIC: American Melody, harm. and arr. by Carlton Young, 1965

CHARLESTOWN
87. 87.

858
And Can It Be That I Should Gain

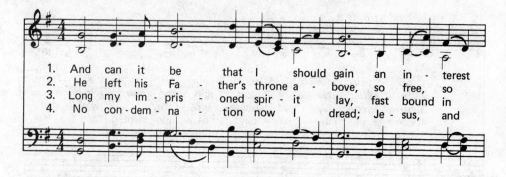

1. And can it be that I should gain an in - terest
2. He left his Fa - ther's throne a - bove, so free, so
3. Long my im - pris - oned spir - it lay, fast bound in
4. No con - dem - na - tion now I dread; Je - sus, and

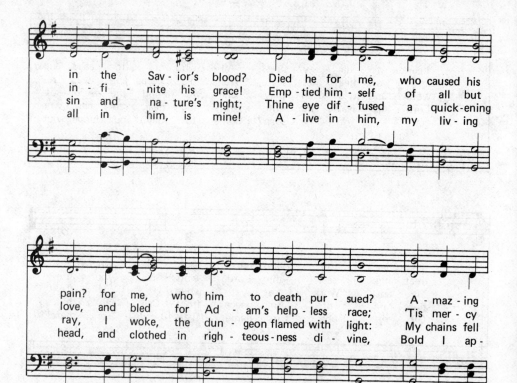

in the Sav - ior's blood? Died he for me, who caused his
in - fi - nite his grace! Emp - tied him - self of all but
sin and na - ture's night; Thine eye dif - fused a quick - ening
all in him, is mine! A - live in him, my liv - ing

pain? for me, who him to death pur - sued? A - maz - ing
love, and bled for Ad - am's help - less race; 'Tis mer - cy
ray, I woke, the dun - geon flamed with light: My chains fell
head, and clothed in righ - teous - ness di - vine, Bold I ap -

WORDS: Charles Wesley, 1738 ; Romans 5:6-11; vs. 2, Phillipians 2:5-7
MUSIC: Arr. from Thomas Campbell

SAGINA
88. 88. 88.

love! how can it be that thou my God, shouldst
all! im - mense and free, that for, O my God, it
off, my heart was free, I rose, went forth, and
proach th'e - ter - nal throne, and claim the crown, through

die for me? A - maz - ing love! how can it
found out me! 'Tis mer - cy all! im - mense and
fol - lowed thee; My chains fell off, my heart was
Christ my own. Bold I ap - proach th'e - ter - nal

1. A - maz - ing love! How
2. 'Tis mer - cy all! im -
3. My chains fell off, my
4. Bold I ap - proach th'e -

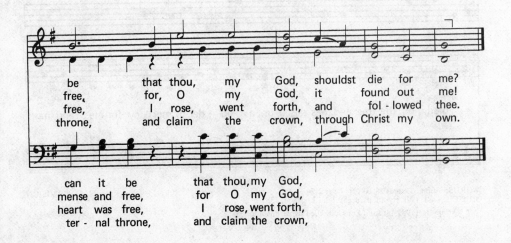

be that thou, my God, shouldst die for me?
free, for, O my God, it found out me!
free, I rose, went forth, and fol - lowed thee.
throne, and claim the crown, through Christ my own.

can it be that thou, my God,
mense and free, for O my God,
heart was free, I rose, went forth,
ter - nal throne, and claim the crown,

859
As Jacob with Travel

As Ja-cob with trav-el was wea-ry one day, at night on a stone for a
pil-low he lay; He saw in a vi-sion a lad-der so high, that its
foot was on earth and its top in the sky. Al-le-lu-ia to Je-sus, who
died on the tree and has raised up a lad-der of mer-cy for me, and has

WORDS: Anon., Genesis 28:10-12; I Peter 2:24
MUSIC: Trad. Folk Hymn; harm. by John Erickson, 1981
Arr. © Copyright 1982 by John Erickson. Used by permission.

JACOB'S VISION
Irregular

raised up a lad - der of mer - cy for me.

860
Amen

**A - men, * a - men,

A - men, O Lawd - y! A - men, have mer - cy!

1. a - men, a - men, a - men. 2. men.

A - men, a - men, a - men. Sing it o - ver now, men.

** Pronounce: AY-MEN.
* Stanzas may be improvised.

WORDS: Trad. Negro Spiritual
MUSIC: Trad. Negro Spiritual, harm. by J. Jefferson Cleveland and Verolga Nix, 1981.

AMEN
Irregular

861
As the Bridegroom to His Chosen

*Unison

1. As the bride-groom to his cho - sen, as the king un - to his
2. As the foun - tain in the gar - den, as the can - dle in the
3. As the mu - sic at the ban - quet, as the stamp un - to the
4. As the ru - by in the set - ting, as the hon - ey in the
5. As the sun - shine in the heav - ens, as the im - age in the

realm, As the keep un - to the cas - tle, as the
dark, As the trea - sure in the cof - fer, as the
seal, As the med - i - cine to the faint - ing, as the
comb, As the light with - in the lan - tern, as the
glass, As the fruit up - on the fig tree, as the

pi - lot to the helm,
man - na in the ark,
wine-cup at the meal, } So, Lord, art thou to me.
fa - ther in the home,
dew up - on the grass,

* NOTE: May be played ½ step lower.

WORDS: John Tauler, 14th cent.; para by Emma Frances Bevan, 1858; Revelation 21:2-3
MUSIC: Peter Cutts, 1969

BRIDEGROOM
87. 87. 6.

Music by permission of Oxford University Press.

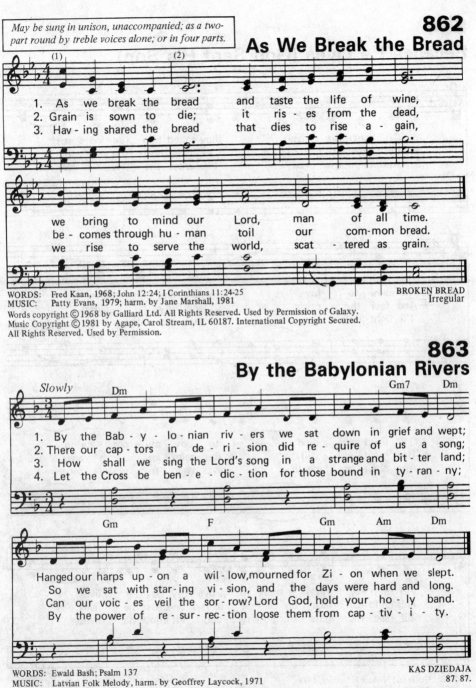

862
As We Break the Bread

May be sung in unison, unaccompanied; as a two-part round by treble voices alone; or in four parts.

1. As we break the bread and taste the life of wine,
2. Grain is sown to die; it ris - es from the dead,
3. Hav - ing shared the bread that dies to rise a - gain,

we bring to mind our Lord, man of all time.
be - comes through hu - man toil our com - mon bread.
we rise to serve the world, scat - tered as grain.

WORDS: Fred Kaan, 1968; John 12:24; I Corinthians 11:24-25
MUSIC: Patty Evans, 1979; harm. by Jane Marshall, 1981

BROKEN BREAD
Irregular

863
By the Babylonian Rivers

Slowly

1. By the Bab - y - lo - nian riv - ers we sat down in grief and wept;
2. There our cap - tors in de - ri - sion did re - quire of us a song;
3. How shall we sing the Lord's song in a strange and bit - ter land;
4. Let the Cross be ben - e - dic - tion for those bound in ty - ran - ny;

Hanged our harps up - on a wil - low, mourned for Zi - on when we slept.
So we sat with star - ing vi - sion, and the days were hard and long.
Can our voic - es veil the sor - row? Lord God, hold your ho - ly band.
By the power of re - sur - rec - tion loose them from cap - tiv - i - ty.

WORDS: Ewald Bash; Psalm 137
MUSIC: Latvian Folk Melody, harm. by Geoffrey Laycock, 1971

KAS DZIEDAJA
87. 87.

864
Because He Lives (God Sent His Son)

1. God sent his Son, they called him Je - sus;
2. How sweet to hold a new-born ba - by,
3. And then one day I'll cross the riv - er;

He came to love, heal, and for - give;
And feel the pride and joy he gives;
I'll fight life's fi - nal war with pain;

He lived and died to buy my par - don,
But great - er still the calm as - sur - ance,
And then as death gives way to vic - tory,

An emp - ty grave is there to prove my Sav - ior lives.
This child can face un - cer - tain days be-cause he lives.
I'll see the lights of glo - ry and I'll know he lives.

WORDS: Gloria and William J. Gaither, 1971
MUSIC: William J. Gaither, 1971

RESURRECTION
Irregular

Be - cause he lives I can face to - mor - row;

Be - cause he lives all fear is gone;

Be - cause I know he holds the fu - ture,

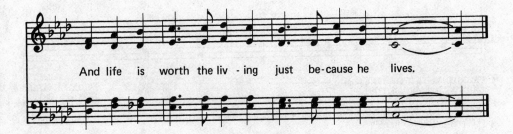

And life is worth the liv - ing just be - cause he lives.

865
Become to Us the Living Bread

May be sung by the choir alone, in parts, during the serving of the bread and wine.

1. Be-come to us the liv-ing bread by which the Chris-tian life
2. Be-come the nev-er-fail-ing wine, the spring of joy that shall
3. May Chris-tians all with one ac-cord u-nite a-round the sa -

is   fed,   re-newed, and great-ly com-fort-ed,
in-cline   our hearts   to bear the cove-nant sign,
cred   board   to praise your ho-ly name, O Lord,

Al - le - lu - ia, al - le - lu - ia!

WORDS: Miriam Drury, 1970; John 6: 53-56
MUSIC: Jane Marshall, 1976

ONE ACCORD
888.with Alleluias

1. Born in the night, Ma-ry's child, a long way from your home; Com-ing in need, Ma-ry's child, born in a bor-rowed room.
2. Clear shin-ing light, Ma-ry's child, your face lights up our way; Light of the world, Ma-ry's child, dawn on our dark-ened day.
3. Truth of our life, Ma-ry's child, you tell us God is good; Prove it is true, Ma-ry's child, go to your cross of wood.
4. Hope of the world, Ma-ry's child, you come a-gain to reign; King of the earth, Ma-ry's child, walk in our streets a-gain.

WORDS and MUSIC: Geoffrey J. Ainger; Luke 2:7
Used by permission of Galaxy.

AINGER
76. 76.

867
By Gracious Powers

This hymn can be accompanied two ways: play lines A and D together, with A in octaves and B pesante, or heavily; or play lines B and C together. It can also be sung by a solo voice, with a flute playing the alto line of the B C setting.

1. By gra-cious powers so won-der-ful-ly shel-ter'd, and con-
2. Yet is this heart by its old foe tor-men-ted, still e-
3. And when this cup you give is filled to brim-ming with bit-
4. Yet when a-gain in this same world you give us the joy

fi-dent-ly wait-ing come what may,   We know that
vil days bring bur-dens hard to bear;   O give our
ter suf-fering, hard to un-der-stand,   We take it
we had, the bright-ness of your sun,   We shall re-

WORDS: Dietrich Bonhoeffer, 1944-45; English version by F. Pratt Green, 1972; Ephesians 5:20
MUSIC: Joseph Gelineau; 1953

BONHOEFFER
11 10. 11 10.

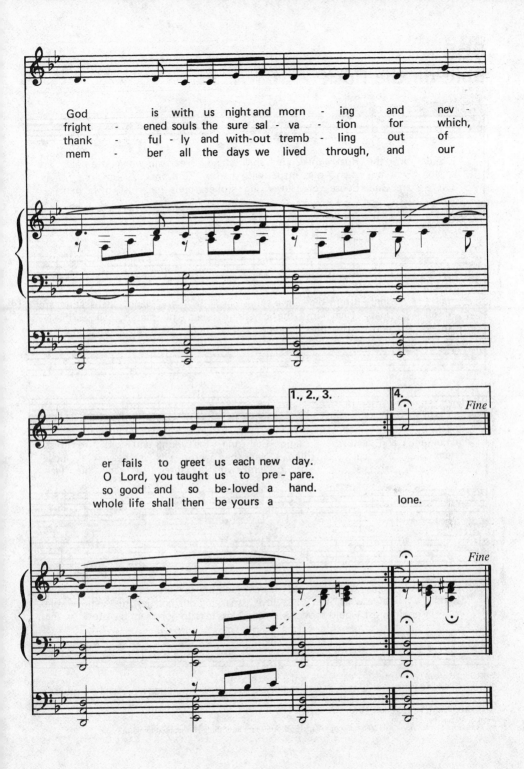

God   is with us night and morn - ing   and   nev -
fright - ened souls the sure sal - va - tion   for   which,
thank - ful - ly and with-out tremb - ling   out   of
mem - ber all the days we lived through, and   our

1., 2., 3.   **4.**   *Fine*

er fails to greet us each new day.
O Lord, you taught us to pre - pare.
so good and so be-loved a hand.
whole life shall then be yours a   lone.

Fine

868
Built on the Rock

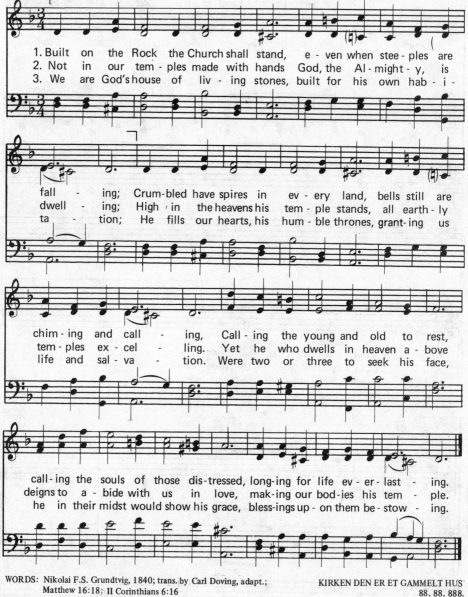

1. Built on the Rock the Church shall stand, e - ven when stee - ples are
2. Not in our tem - ples made with hands God, the Al - might - y, is
3. We are God's house of liv - ing stones, built for his own hab - i -

fall - ing; Crum-bled have spires in ev - ery land, bells still are
dwell - ing; High in the heavens his tem - ple stands, all earth - ly
ta - tion; He fills our hearts, his hum - ble thrones, grant - ing us

chim - ing and call - ing, Call - ing the young and old to rest,
tem - ples ex - cel - ling. Yet he who dwells in heaven a - bove
life and sal - va - tion. Were two or three to seek his face,

call - ing the souls of those dis - tressed, long-ing for life ev - er - last - ing.
deigns to a - bide with us in love, mak-ing our bod-ies his tem - ple.
he in their midst would show his grace, bless-ings up - on them be - stow - ing.

WORDS: Nikolai F.S. Grundtvig, 1840; trans. by Carl Doving, adapt.;
    Matthew 16:18; II Corinthians 6:16
MUSIC: Ludvig M. Lindeman, 1840

KIRKEN DEN ER ET GAMMELT HUS
88. 88. 888.

Christ, upon the Mountain Peak

♩=60

1. Christ, up - on the moun-tain peak, stands a - lone in glo - ry
2. Trem - bling at his feet we saw Mo - ses and E - li - jah
3. Swift the cloud of glo - ry came, God pro-claim - ing in its
4. This is God's be - lov - ed Son! Law and proph-ets fade be -

blaz - ing; Let us, if we dare to speak,
speak - ing. All the proph - ets and the law
thun - der Je - sus as his Son by name!
fore him; First and last and on - ly one,

with the saints and an - gels praise him.
shout through them their joy - ful greet - ing. Al - le - lu - ia!
Na - tions, cry a - loud in won - der
let cre - a - tion now a - dore him.

WORDS: Brian A. Wren, 1962; Mark 9:2-8
MUSIC: Peter Cutts, 1963   Alternate tune: LIEBSTER JESU (BOH 257)
Words and music by permission of Oxford University Press.

SHILLINGFORD
78. 78. with Alleluia

870
Christ Is Alive

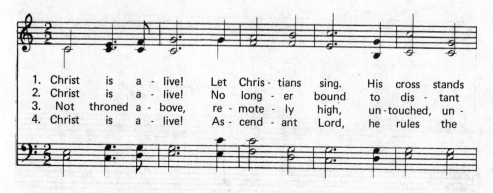

1. Christ is a - live! Let Chris - tians sing. His cross stands
2. Christ is a - live! No long - er bound to dis - tant
3. Not throned a - bove, re - mote - ly high, un - touched, un -
4. Christ is a - live! As - cend - ant Lord, he rules the

emp - ty to the sky. Let streets and homes with
years in Pal - es - tine, He comes to claim the
moved by hu - man pains, But dai - ly, in the
world his Fa - ther made, Till in the end his

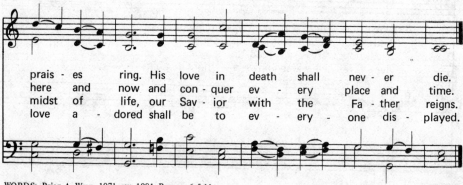

prais - es ring. His love in death shall nev - er die.
here and now and con - quer ev - er - y place and time.
midst of life, our Sav - ior with the Fa - ther reigns.
love a - dored shall be to ev - er - y - one dis - played.

WORDS: Brian A. Wren, 1971, rev. 1981; Romans 6:5-11
MUSIC: T. Williams' *Psalmodia Evangelica*, 1789
Words used by permission of Oxford Univeristy Press.

TRURO
LM

Christian People, Raise Your Song

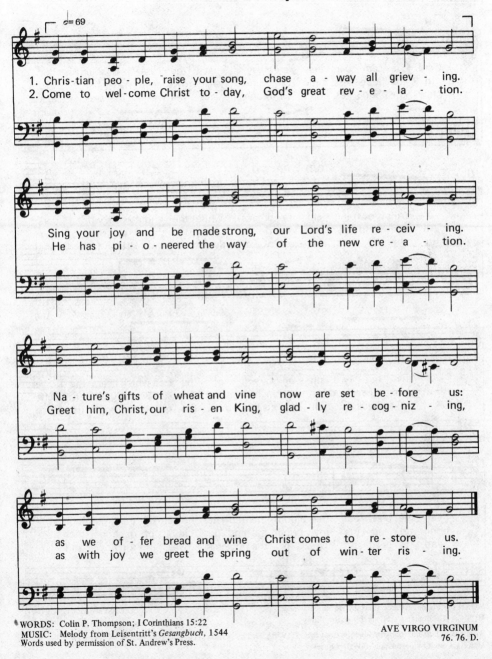

1. Chris-tian peo-ple, raise your song, chase a-way all griev-ing.
2. Come to wel-come Christ to-day, God's great rev-e-la-tion.

Sing your joy and be made strong, our Lord's life re-ceiv-ing.
He has pi-o-neered the way of the new cre-a-tion.

Na-ture's gifts of wheat and vine now are set be-fore us:
Greet him, Christ, our ris-en King, glad-ly re-cog-niz-ing,

as we of-fer bread and wine Christ comes to re-store us.
as with joy we greet the spring out of win-ter ris-ing.

WORDS: Colin P. Thompson; I Corinthians 15:22
MUSIC: Melody from Leisentritt's *Gesangbuch*, 1544
Words used by permission of St. Andrew's Press.

AVE VIRGO VIRGINUM
76. 76. D.

872
Cold December Flies Away

1. Cold De-cem-ber flies a-way at the rose-red splen-dor.
2. In the hope-less time of sin shad-ows deep had fall-en.
3. Now the bud has come to bloom, and the world a-wak-ens.

A-pril's crown-ing glo-ry breaks while the whole world won-ders
All the world lay un-der death, eyes were closed in sleep-ing.
In the lil-y's pur-est flower dwells a won-drous fra-grance.

At the ho-ly un-seen power of the tree which bears the flower.
But, when all seemed lost in night, came the sun whose gold-en light
And it spreads to all the earth from the mo-ment of its birth;

On the bless-ed tree blooms the red-dest flower, on the tree blooms the
brings un-end-ing joy, brings the end-less joy of our hope, high-est
and its beau-ty lives. In the flower it lives, in the flower and it

WORDS: Catalonian Carol, trans. by Howard Hawhee
MUSIC: Catalonian Carol; arr. by Walter Ehret

LO DESEMBRE CONGELAT
Irregular

Words from *Lutheran Book of Worship*, Copyright © 1978. Used by permission of Augsburg Publishing House.
Music arr. used by permission of Walter Ehret

rose here in love's own gar - den, full and strong in glo - ry.
hope, of our hope's bright dawn - ing, Son be - loved of heav - en.
spreads in its heaven - ly bright - ness sweet per - fume de - light - ful.

873
Cup of Blessing That We Share

Unison

1. Cup of bless - ing that we share, does it not his grace de - clare?
2. Is it not one bread we break? Of his bod - y all par - take.

Is it not the blood of Christ, who for us was sac - ri - ficed?
Cast - ing out dis - trust and fear, let us love with hearts sin - cere.

As one bod - y, we are fed; Christ we share, one cup, one bread.
One by God's de - sign are we; let us live in u - ni - ty.

WORDS: Bernard Mischke, 1966; John 17:22-23
MUSIC: Knut Nystedt, 1972

TORSHOV
77. 77. 77.

874
Come, Ye Sinners, Poor and Needy

Unison

1. Come, ye sinners, poor and needy,
2. Come, ye thirst-y, come, and wel-come,
3. Come, ye wea-ry, heav-y-la-den,
4. Let not con-science make you lin-ger,

Refrain: I will a-rise and go to Je-sus,

weak and wound-ed, sick and sore; Je-sus read-y
God's free boun-ty glo-ri-fy; True be-lief and
lost and ru-ined by the fall; If you tar-ry
nor of fit-ness fond-ly dream; All the fit-ness

he will em-brace me in his arms; In the arms of

stands to save you, full of pit-y, love, and power.
true re-pent-ance, ev-ery grace that brings you nigh.
till you're bet-ter, you will nev-er come at all.
he re-quir-eth is to feel your need of him.

my dear Sav-ior, O there are ten thou-sand charms.

WORDS: Joseph Hart, 1759, Refrain, Anon.; Matthew 11:28-29
MUSIC: *Southern Harmony*, 1835; harm. & arr. by Carlton Young, 1982
Arr. copyright © 1982 by Carlton Young. Used by permission.

RESTORATION
8 7. 8 7.

(874-a)

High voices   RESTORATION, Shape Note Version

1. Come,   ye   sin - ners,   poor   and   need - y,
2. Come,   ye   thirst - y,   come,   and   wel - come,
3. Come,   ye   wea - ry,   heav - y - la - den,
4. Let   not   con - science   make   you   lin - ger,
Refrain: I   will a - rise   and   go   to   Je - sus,

Melody

1. Come,   ye   sin - ners,   poor   and   need - y,
2. Come,   ye   thirst - y,   come,   and   wel - come,
3. Come,   ye   wea - ry,   heav - y - la - den,
4. Let   not   con - science   make   you   lin - ger,
Refrain: I   will a - rise   and   go   to   Je - sus,

Low voices

1. Come,   ye   sin - ners,   poor   and   need - y,
2. Come,   ye   thirst - y,   come,   and   wel - come,
3. Come,   ye   wea - ry,   heav - y - la - den,
4. Let   not   con - science   make   you   lin - ger,
Refrain: I   will a - rise   and   go   to   Je - sus.

(874-b)

weak and wound - ed, sick and sore; Je - sus read - y
God's free boun - ty glo - ri - fy; True be - lief and
lost and ru - ined by the fall; If you tar - ry
nor of fit - ness fond - ly dream; All the fit - ness
He will em - brace me in his arms; In the arms of

weak and wound - ed, sick and sore; Je - sus read - y
God's free boun - ty glo - ri - fy; True be - lief and
lost and ru - ined by the fall; If you tar - ry
nor of fit - ness fond - ly dream; All the fit - ness
He will em - brace me in his arms; In the arms of

weak and wound - ed, sick and sore; Je - sus read - y
God's free boun - ty glo - ri - fy; True be - lief and
lost and ru - ined by the fall; If you tar - ry
nor of fit - ness fond - ly dream; All the fit - ness
He will em - brace me in his arms; In the arms of

(874-c)

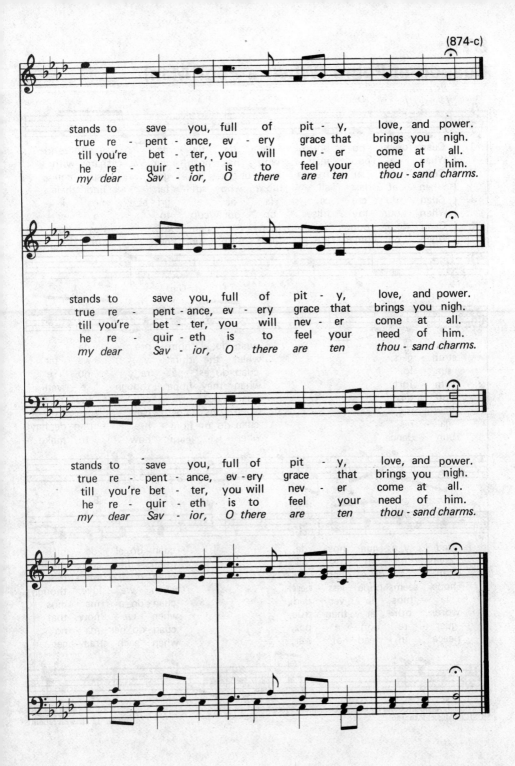

stands to   save   you, full   of   pit - y,   love, and power.
true re - pent - ance, ev - ery   grace that   brings you nigh.
till you're bet - ter, you will   nev - er   come at all.
he re - quir - eth is   to   feel your   need of him.
my dear   Sav - ior, O there are ten   thou - sand charms.

stands to   save   you, full   of   pit - y,   love, and power.
true re - pent - ance, ev - ery   grace that   brings you nigh.
till you're bet - ter, you will   nev - er   come at all.
he re - quir - eth is   to   feel your   need of him.
my dear   Sav - ior, O there   are ten   thou - sand charms.

stands to   save   you, full of   pit - y,   love, and power.
true re - pent - ance, ev - ery   grace   that   brings you nigh.
till you're bet - ter, you will   nev - er   come at all.
he re - quir - eth is   to   feel   your   need of him.
my dear Sav - ior, O there   are   ten   thou - sand charms.

875

Cuando el Pobre (When a Poor Man)

Estrofa.
[Verses:]

1. { Cuan-do_el po - bre na - da tie - na y_aun re -
   { When a poor man who has noth - ing shares with
2. { Cuan - do su - fre_un hom-bre_y lo - gra su con -
   { When at last all those who suf - fer find their
3. { Cuan - do cre - ce la al - e - grí - a_y nos i -
   { When our joy fills up our cup to o - ver -
4. { Cuan-do_a bun - da_el bien y llen - a los ho -
   { When our homes are filled with good - ness in a -

par - te, cuan-do_el hom - bre pa - sa
stran - gers, when the thirst - y wa - ter
sue - lo, cuan-do_es - pa - ra_y no se
com - fort, when they hope though e - ven
nun - da, cuan - do di - cen nues - tros
flow - ing, when our lips can speak no
ga - res, cuan-do_un hom - bre don-de_hay
bun - dance, when we learn how to make

sed y_a - gua nos da, cuan-do_el dé - bil
give un - to us all, when the crip - ple
can - sa de_es-per - ar, cuan-do_a - ma - mos,
hope seems hope - less - ness, when we love though
la - bios la ver - dad, cuan-do_a - ma - mos
words oth - er than true, when we know that
guer - ra pon - e paz, cuan-do_"her - ma - no"
peace in - stead of war, when each stran - ger

WORDS: J. A. Olivar; trans. by George Lockwood, 1980
MUSIC: Miguel Manzano

THE ROAD
12 11. 12 11. with refrain

876
DAW-KEE,
AIM DAW-TSI
(Great Spirit, Now I Pray)

Freely, like a chant

DAW - KEE, AIM DAW - TSI TO - AW - BAY TAH HAAL
Great Spir - it, now I pray to you, I

DAW - KEE, AIM DAW - TSI TO - AW - BAY TAH HAAL
pray now to you, Great Spir - it, hear me;

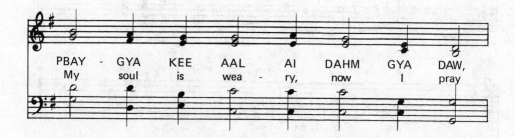

PBAY - GYA KEE AAL AI DAHM GYA DAW,
My soul is wea - ry, now I pray

WORDS: Kiowa Prayer; English para. by Libby Littlechief, 1980 ; Romans 8:9-11
MUSIC: Native American; arr. by Charles Boynton, 1980

KIOWA
10 10. 8 8.

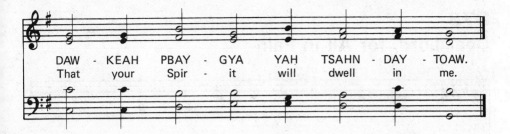

DAW - KEAH PBAY - GYA YAH TSAHN - DAY - TOAW.
That your Spir - it will dwell in me.

877
Demos Gracias al Señor
(We Give Thanks Unto the Lord)

De - mos gra - cias al Se - ñor, De - mos gra - cias, De - mos gra - cias por su a-
We give thanks un-to the Lord, we say, "Thank you," We say, "Thank you for your

mor. Por la ma - ña - na las a - ves can - tan sus a - la -
love." For in the morn-ing the birds are sing-ing their prais - es

ban- zas a Dios el Cre - a - dor. Tam-bién no - so - tros a Él can-
to God, Cre-a-tor of us all. So let us al - so to him bring

te - mos y a - la - be - mos al Cris-to el Re - den - tor.
sing-ing and prais - es, to Christ, Re-deem-er of us all.

WORDS: Trad. Hispanic; English trans. by Esther Frances, 1978; Psalm 118:29
MUSIC: Arr. by Esther Frances, 1978
Arr. & trans. copyright © 1979 by Esther Frances. Used by permission.

DEMOS GRACIAS
Irregular

878
Dear Lord, for All in Pain

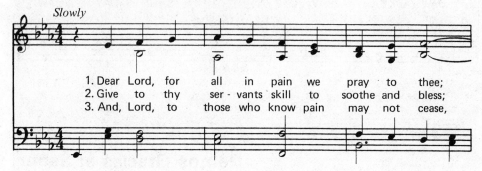

Slowly

1. Dear Lord, for all in pain we pray to thee;
2. Give to thy ser-vants skill to soothe and bless;
3. And, Lord, to those who know pain may not cease,

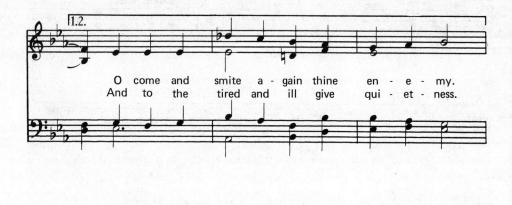

O come and smite a-gain thine en-e-my.
And to the tired and ill give qui-et-ness.

Come near, that e-ven so they may have peace.

WORDS: Amy W. Carmichael, 1931; Psalm 69:29
MUSIC: K. D. Smith, 1928
Words reprinted from the *Anglican Hymnbook;* used by permission of the Society for Promoting Christian Knowledge.
Music reprinted from the *Anglican Hymnbook,* used by permission of the Church Society.

RAPHAEL
64. 64.

Descend, O Spirit, Purging Flame

1. De - scend, O Spir - it, purg - ing flame, brand us this
2. Wash us with wa - ter, make us pure; thrust us in
3. For - bid us not this sec - ond birth; grant un - to

day with Je - sus' name! Con - firm our faith, con -
mis - sion to en - dure. Let now your heal - ing
us the great - er worth! Con - script us in your

sume our doubt; sign us as Christ's, with - in, with - out.
wa - ters win new life, new hope, re - lease from sin.
serv - ice, Lord; bap - tize all na - tions with your Word.

WORDS: Scott Francis Brenner, 1969; Acts 19:1-6
MUSIC: Griffith Hugh Jones, 1890, arr. by Donald D. Kettring, 1972

LLEF
LM

880
Earth and All Stars

May be sung in unison or in parts, antiphonally.

In one

1. Earth and all stars, loud rush - ing plan - ets
2. Hail, wind, and rain, loud blow - ing snow - storm
3. Trum - pet and pipes, loud clash - ing cym - bals
4. Class - rooms and labs, loud boil - ing test - tubes
5. Knowl - edge and truth, loud sound - ing wis - dom

Sing to the Lord a new song!

1. O vic - to - ry, loud shout - ing ar - my
2. Flow - ers and trees, loud rus - tling dry leaves
3. Harp, lute, and lyre, loud hum - ming cel - los
4. Ath - lete and band, loud cheer - ing peo - ple
5. Daugh - ter and son, loud pray - ing mem - bers

Sing to the Lord a new song! He hath done mar

WORDS: Herbert F. Brokering, 1968
MUSIC: David N. Johnson, 1968

DEXTER
Irregular with Refrain

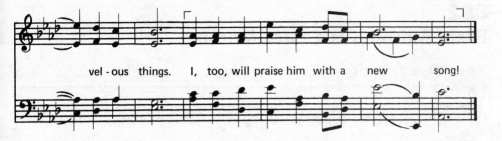

vel - ous things. I, too, will praise him with a new song!

881
Fill My Cup, Lord

Freely

Fill my cup, Lord, I lift it up, Lord. Come and

quench this thirst-ing of my soul. Bread of heav-en, feed me till I

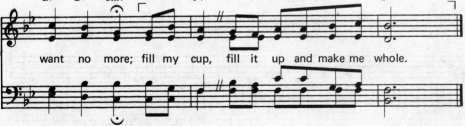

want no more; fill my cup, fill it up and make me whole.

WORDS: Richard Blanchard, 1959; John 4:7-15, 6:51
MUSIC: Richard Blanchard, arr. by Eugene Clark, 1971

FILL MY CUP
Irregular

882
Every Morning Is Easter Morning

Ev - 'ry morn-ing is   Eas-ter Morn-ing   from now on!

Ev - 'ry day's Res - ur-rec - tion Day, the   past   is   o - ver and gone!

1. Good - bye guilt, good-bye fear, good rid - dance! Hel - lo Lord, hel - lo   sun!
2. Dai - ly news is so bad   it seems the Good News sel - dom gets heard.
3. Yes - ter - day I was bored and lone - ly; But to-day look and see!

I am   one   of the Eas-ter Peo-ple! My new life   has be - gun!
Get it straight from the Eas-ter Peo-ple: God's in charge! Spread the word!
I be - long   to the Eas-ter Peo-ple! Life's ex - cit - ing to

me!   Ev - 'ry morn-ing is Eas - ter Morn-ing from now on!

WORDS and MUSIC: Richard K. Avery and Donald S. Marsh, 1972 ; Romans 6:1-4

EASTER MORNING
Irregular
with Coda

Ev -'ry day's Res- ur - rec -tion Day, the past is o - ver and gone!

p Ev -'ry morn-ing is Eas-ter Morn-ing, *pp* Ev -'ry morn-ing is Eas-ter Morn-ing,

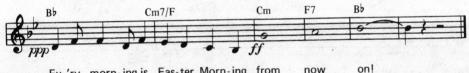

ppp Ev -'ry morn-ing is Eas-ter Morn-ing *ff* from now on!

883
For You Shall Go out in Joy

Gently, with freedom

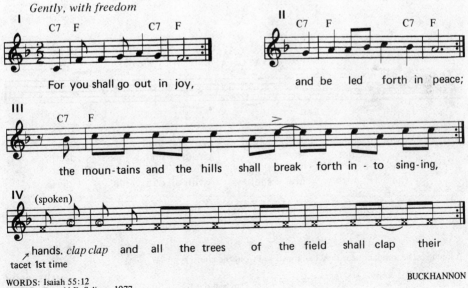

I
C7 F   C7 F
For you shall go out in joy,

II
C7 F   C7 F
and be led forth in peace;

III
C7 F
the moun-tains and the hills shall break forth in - to sing-ing,

IV (spoken)
hands. *clap clap* and all the trees of the field shall clap their
tacet 1st time

BUCKHANNON

WORDS: Isaiah 55:12
MUSIC: Donald E. Saliers, 1977

884

Father, I Stretch My Hands to Thee

Very slowly

1. Fa - ther, I stretch my hands to thee; no oth -
2. What did thine on - ly Son en - dure, be - fore
3. Sure - ly thou canst not let me die, O speak
4. Au - thor of faith! to thee I lift my wea -

er help I know; If thou with - draw thy - self
I drew my breath! What pain, what la - bor to
and I shall live; And here I will un - wea -
ry, long - ing eyes; O let me now re - ceive

from me, Ah! whith - er shall I go?
se - cure my soul from end - less death!
ried lie till thou thy spir - it give.
that gift! My soul with - out it dies.

A keyboard accompaniment may be improvised from the chord symbols.

WORDS: Charles Wesley, 1741; John 6:68
MUSIC: Hugh Wilson, 18th cent.; lined by J. Jefferson Cleveland and Verolga Nix, 1981

MARTYRDOM
CM

Faith, While Trees Are Still in Blossom

♩=80

1. Faith, while trees are still in blos - som,
2. Long be - fore the dawn is break - ing,
3. Long be - fore the rains were com - ing
4. Faith, up - lift - ed, tamed the wa - ter
5. Faith be - lieves that God is faith - ful,

plans the pick - ing of the fruit; faith can feel the
faith an - ti - ci - pates the sun. Faith is ea - ger
No - ah went and built an ark. A - bra - ham, the
of the un - di - vid - ed sea, and the peo - ple
He will be that he will be! Faith ac - cepts his

thrill of har - vest when the buds be - gin to sprout.
for the day - light, for the work that must be done.
lone - ly mi - grant, saw the Light be - yond the dark.
of the He - brews found the path that made them free.
call, re - spond - ing: "I am will - ing, Lord, send me."

WORDS: Anders Frostenson, 1960; trans. by Fred Kaan, 1972; Hebrews 11:1-2
MUSIC: Alec Wyton. 1977

FAITH
87. 87.

Words copyright by Ansgar Film & Bokproduktion. Used by permission. Words copyright ©1976 by Stainer & Bell, Ltd.
All Rights Reserved. Used by Permission of Galaxy. Music Copyright © 1977 by Agape, Carol Stream, IL 60187.
International Copyright Secured. All Rights Reserved. Used by Permission.
Alternate tune: KINGDOM (BOH 314)

886
From the Slave Pens of the Delta

1. "From the slave pens of the Del - ta, from the ghet - tos
2. "From the ag - ing shrines and struc - tures, from the clois - ter
3. When we mur - mur on the moun - tains for the old E -
4. In the mael - strom of the na - tions, in the jour - neying

on the Nile, Let my peo - ple seek their free - dom
and the aisle, Let my peo - ple seek their free - dom
gyp - tian plains, When we miss our an - cient bond - age
in - to space, In the clash of gen - er - a - tions,

in the wil - der - ness a - while": So God spake from out of
in the wil - der - ness a - while": So the Son of God has
and the hope, the prom - ise, wanes, Then the rock shall yield its
in the hun - ger - ing for grace, In our ag - o - ny and

WORDS: T. Herbert O'Driscoll ; Deuteronomy 8:14-18
MUSIC: Thomas J. Williams, 1890
Words used by permission of Herbert O'Driscoll.
Music used by permission of Gwenlyn Evans, Ltd.

EBENEZER
87. 87. D

Si - nai, so God spake and it was done, And God's peo - ple
spo - ken, and the storm - clouds are un - furled, For God's peo - ple
wa - ter and the man - na fall by night, And with vi - sions
glo - ry, we are called to new - er ways By the Lord of

crossed the wa - ters toward the ris - ing of the sun.
must be scat - tered to be ser - vants in the world.
of a fu - ture shall we march to - ward the light.
our to - mor - rows and the God of earth's to - days.

887
Father, I Adore You

Round

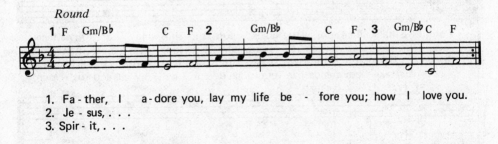

1. Fa - ther, I a - dore you, lay my life be - fore you; how I love you.
2. Je - sus, . . .
3. Spir - it, . . .

WORDS and MUSIC: Terrye Coelho, 1972

ABBA
Irregular

888
Fount of Love, Our Savior God

1. Fount of love, our Sav-ior God, light on baf-fling ways we've trod,
2. In this time of sore dis-tress, hid-den dan-gers round us press;
3. Life is bur-dened down with care, dreams like bub-bles burst in air;
4. Man-y paths be-fore us lie, man-y voic-es to us cry;

Cross of Christ—a com-pass sure, love of Christ—the vi-sion pure:
Life's true way we can-not find, fears and fan-cies fill the mind.
Hu-man hopes are emp-ty things, like dead trees and dried-up springs;
Which of all these shall we choose? here find gain or there all lose.

Lord, we thank thee for thy grace, for the shin-ing of thy face.
Sav-ior, give us eyes to see thy great king-dom that shall be.
Grant us, Prince of Life, we pray, life a-bun-dant ev-ery day.
Je-sus, take our hands in thine, guide us by thy grand de-sign.

WORDS: Ernest Y. L. Yang; trans. by Frank W. Price
MUSIC: Ancient Chinese; arr. by Roger Vuataz, 1951

CHINA
77. 77. D.

889
Glory Be to the Father (Gloria Patri)

Glo-ry be to the Fa-ther, glo-ry be to the Son, glo-ry be to the Ho-ly Ghost, Three in One; as it was in the be-gin-ning, is now, and shall be, world with-out end. A-men.

WORDS: Lesser Doxology (Gloria Patri) c. 4th cent.
MUSIC: John Erickson, 1969

ERICKSON

890
Give Me a Clean Heart

Give me a clean heart so I may serve thee. Lord, fix my heart so that I may be used by

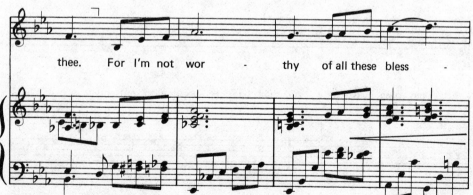

thee. For I'm not wor - thy of all these bless -

WORDS: Margaret Douroux, 1970 ; Psalm 51:10
MUSIC: Margaret Douroux; arr. by Albert Denis Tessier

CLEAN HEART
Irregular

ings. Give me a clean heart and I'll fol-low thee.

1. I'm not ask - ing for the rich - es of the land.
   I am up and some-times I am down.

I'm not ask - ing for high men to know my name.
Some-times I am al - most lev - el to the ground.

(890-b)

Please give me, Lord, a clean heart, that I may fol - low
Please give me, Lord, a clean heart, that I may fol - low

thee. Give me a clean heart, a clean heart and
thee. Give me a clean heart, a clean heart and

I will fol - low thee.
I will fol - low thee.

2. Some - times

891
God Is So Good

D   A   D

1. God is so good, God is so good,

D7   G   D/A   A7   D

God is so good, He's so good to me.

2. He cares for me, . . .   3. I'll do his will, . . .   4. He loves me so, . . .

WORDS and MUSIC: Anon., 20th cent.

GOOD
Irregular

892
God Is Working His Purpose Out

1. God is work - ing his pur - pose out as
2. From ut - most east to ut - most west, wher -
3. March we forth in the strength of God, with the
4. All we can do is noth - ing worth un -

year suc - ceeds to year: God is work - ing his
ev - er man's foot hath trod, By the mouth of man - y
ban - ner of Christ un - furled, That the light of the glo - rious
less God bless - es the deed; Vain - ly we hope for the

pur - pose out, and the time is draw - ing near;
mes - sen - gers goes forth the voice of God;
gos - pel of truth may shine through-out the world;
har - vest - tide till God gives life to the seed; Yet

WORDS: Arthur Campbell Ainger, 1894, 1904; Numbers 14:21; John 11:40
MUSIC: Martin Shaw, 1931

PURPOSE
Irregular

Music from *Enlarged Songs of Praise*, by permission of Oxford University Press.

893
Go in Peace
(Gehe ein in deinen, Frieden)

May be sung antiphonally by groups I and II; may be sung one step lower.

Go in peace, and God be with you; sleep in peace, God hold you fast!
Ge - he ein in dei - nen Frie - den! Schla - fe dei - nen gu - ten Schlaf!

Take your ease from dai - ly du - ty; af - ter la - bor rest at last!
Ruh dich aus nach dei - ner Ar - beit, und ge - seg - net sei die Nacht!

Moon - light shares a glimpse of heav - en's mirth, dew - fall fresh - ens
Mond - licht fliesst her - ab vom Him - mels - zelt, und der Tau glänzt

flow - ers of earth. Thank God for day and night. Thank God
auf un - serm Feld. Preist den Tag und die Nacht! Preist die

for dark and light. For the sun and for all things liv - ing
Nacht und den Tag! Preist die Son - ne, prei - set die Er - de,

WORDS: Orig. German text: Helmut Koenig; Psalm 74:16
MUSIC: Israeli tune adapt. by Helmut Koenig

KOENIG
Irregular

Used with permission of Voggenreiter Verlages, Bad Godesberg, West Germany.

to their Lord prais-es giv-ing. A - men. A - men.
preist den Hern al - ler Wel - ten.

894
Go Now in Peace

Keyboard, Handbells
and/or Orff Instruments

Go now in peace, go now in peace, may the love of

God sur - round you ev - ery-where, ev - ery-where you may go.

ORFF INSTRUMENT PATTERNS

1 Alto Glockenspiel 2 Metallophone   3 Alto Xylophone   4 Bass Xylophone

WORDS and MUSIC: Natalie Sleeth, 1976; Luke 2:29   BETTY

895
Great Is Thy Faithfulness

1. Great is thy faith - ful - ness, O God my Fa - ther, There is no
2. Sum - mer and win - ter and spring - time and har - vest, Sun, moon, and
3. Par - don for sin and a peace that en - dur - eth, Thine own dear

shad - ow of turn - ing with thee; Thou chang - est not, thy com -
stars in their cours - es a - bove Join with all na - ture in
pres - ence to cheer and to guide; Strength for to - day and bright

pas - sions, they fail not; As thou hast been thou for - ev - er wilt be.
man - i - fold wit - ness To thy great faith - ful - ness, mer - cy, and love.
hope for to - mor - row, Bless - ings all mine, with ten thou - sand be - side!

WORDS: Thomas O. Chisholm, 1923 ; Lamentations 3:22-23
MUSIC: William M. Runyan, 1923
Copyright 1923. Renewal 1951 extended by Hope Publishing Co., Carol Stream, IL 60187.
All Rights Reserved. Used by Permission.

FAITHFULNESS
11 10. 11 10.
with Refrain

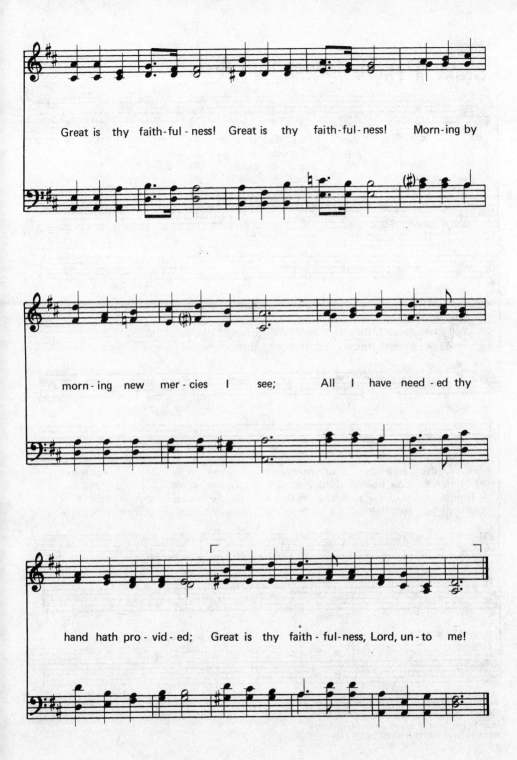

Great is thy faith-ful-ness! Great is thy faith-ful-ness! Morn-ing by

morn-ing new mer-cies I see; All I have need-ed thy

hand hath pro-vid-ed; Great is thy faith-ful-ness, Lord, un-to me!

896
Hail the Day That Sees Him Rise

1. Hail the day that sees him rise, Al - le - lu - ia!
2. There for him high tri - umph waits; Al - le - lu - ia!
3. Lo! the heaven its Lord re - ceives, Al - le - lu - ia!
4. See! he lifts his hands a - bove; Al - le - lu - ia!

To his throne a - bove the skies; Al - le - lu - ia!
Lift your heads, e - ter - nal gates; Al - le - lu - ia!
Yet he loves the earth he leaves; Al - le - lu - ia!
See! he shows the prints of love; Al - le - lu - ia!

Christ, the Lamb for sin - ners given, en - ters now the high - est heaven.
He hath con - quered death and sin; take the King of glo - ry in.
Though re - turn - ing to his throne, still he calls us as his own.
Hark! his gra - cious lips be - stow bless - ings on his church be - low.

Al - le - lu - ia! Al - le - lu - ia! Al - le - lu - ia!

WORDS: Charles Wesley, 1739, Thomas Cotterill, 1820, and others; Psalm 24:9; John 20:17
MUSIC: Sydney Hugo Nicholson
Music by permission of *Hymns Ancient and Modern*
Alternate tune: EASTER HYMN (BOH 439)

CHISLEHURST
77. 77. with Alleluias

This gentle unison hymn is effective if the first three stanzas are sung alternately by choir and congregation and the fourth is sung by all.

Have No Fear, Little Flock

Not fast

1. Have no fear, lit - tle flock, have no
2. Have good cheer, lit - tle flock, have good
3. Praise the Lord high a - bove, praise the
4. Thank - ful hearts raise to God, thank - ful

fear, lit - tle flock, for the Fa - ther has cho - sen to
cheer, lit - tle flock, for the Fa - ther will keep you in
Lord high a - bove, for he stoops down to heal you, up -
hearts raise to God, for he stays close be - side you, in

give you the king - dom. Have no fear, lit - tle flock!
his love for - ev - er. Have good cheer, lit - tle flock!
lift and re - store you. Praise the Lord high a - bove!
all things works with you. Thank - ful hearts raise to God!

WORDS: Luke 12:32, add. verses, Marjorie Jillson, 1972
MUSIC: Heinz Werner Zimmermann, 1971

LITTLE FLOCK
Irregular

898

He Is Born
(Il Est Né)

He is born, the ho - ly Child, play the o - boe and bag-pipes mer-ri - ly!
Il est né, le di - vin En - fant, jou - ez haut-bois, re - son - nez mu - set - tes!

Fine

He is born, the ho - ly Child, sing we all of the Sav - ior mild.
Il est né, le di - vin En - fant, chan - tons tous son a - vé - ne - ment!

1. Through long a - ges of the past, proph-ets have fore - told his com - ing;
2. O how love - ly, O how pure, is this per - fect Child of Heav - en;
3. Je - sus, Lord of all the world, com - ing as a child a - mong us,

D.C.

Through long a - ges of the past; now the time has come at last!
O how love - ly, O how pure, gra - cious gift to hu - man - kind!
Je - sus, Lord of all the world, grant to us thy heaven - ly peace;

WORDS: Trad. 19th cent. French; trans. Anon; Luke 2:7
MUSIC: 18th cent. French Carol; harm. by Norman K. Giesbrecht

IL EST NÉ
Irregular

Harmonization used by permission of Norman K. Giesbrecht and the Baptist Federation of Canada.

899
Help Us Accept Each Other

In a slow two

1. Help us ac-cept each oth-er as Christ ac-cept-ed us;
2. Teach us, O Lord, your les-sons, as in our dai-ly life
3. Let your ac-cept-ance change us, so that we may be moved
4. Lord, for to-day's en-coun-ters with all who are in need,

teach us as sis-ter, broth-er, each per-son to em-brace.
we strug-gle to be hu-man and search for hope and faith.
in liv-ing sit-u-a-tions to do the truth in love;
who hun-ger for ac-cept-ance, for righ-teous-ness and bread,

Be pres-ent, Lord, a-mong us, and bring us to be-lieve
Teach us to care for peo-ple, for all, not just for some;
to prac-tice your ac-cept-ance, un-til we know by heart
we need new eyes for see-ing, new hands for hold-ing on;

we are our-selves ac-cept-ed and meant to love and live.
to love them as we find them, or, as they may be-come.
the ta-ble of for-give-ness and laugh-ter's heal-ing art.
re-new us with your Spir-it; Lord, free us, make us one!

WORDS: Fred Kaan, 1974 ; John 15:12
MUSIC: John Ness Beck; 1977

ACCEPTANCE
76. 76.D.

900

Hosana (Mantles and Branches)

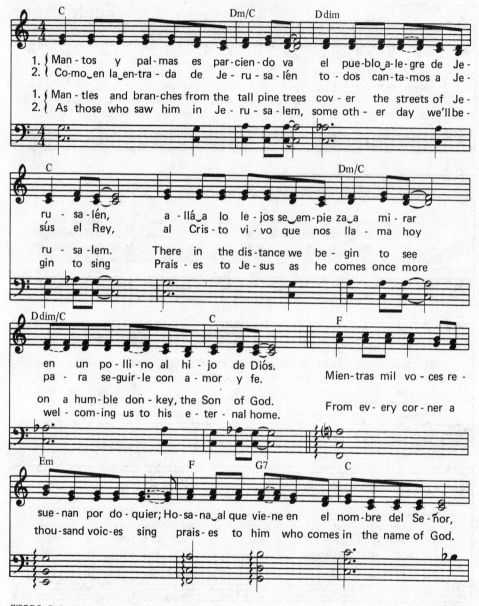

1. Man - tos y pal - mas es par - cien - do va el pue - blo a - le - gre de Je -
2. Co - mo en la en - tra - da de Je - ru - sa - lén to - dos can - ta - mos a Je -

1. Man - tles and bran - ches from the tall pine trees cov - er the streets of Je -
2. As those who saw him in Je - ru - sa - lem, some oth - er day we'll be -

ru - sa - lén, a - llá a lo le - jos se em - pie za a mi - rar
sús el Rey, al Cris - to vi - vo que nos lla - ma hoy

ru - sa - lem. There in the dis - tance we be - gin to see
gin to sing Prais - es to Je - sus as he comes once more

en un po - lli - no al hi - jo de Diós.
pa - ra se - guir - le con a - mor y fe.

on a hum - ble don - key, the Son of God.
wel - com - ing us to his e - ter - nal home.

Mien - tras mil vo - ces re -

From ev - ery cor - ner a

sue - nan por do - quier; Ho - sa - na al que vie - ne en el nom - bre del Se - ñor,
thou - sand voic - es sing prais - es to him who comes in the name of God.

WORDS: Ruben Ruiz Trans. by Gertrude C. Suppe, 1979

MUSIC: Ruben Ruiz

HOSANA
10 9. 10 10. with Refrain

901
How Good to
Offer Thanks

Let the congregation sing the antiphon
(refrain) and a soloist or unison choir sing
the two verses.

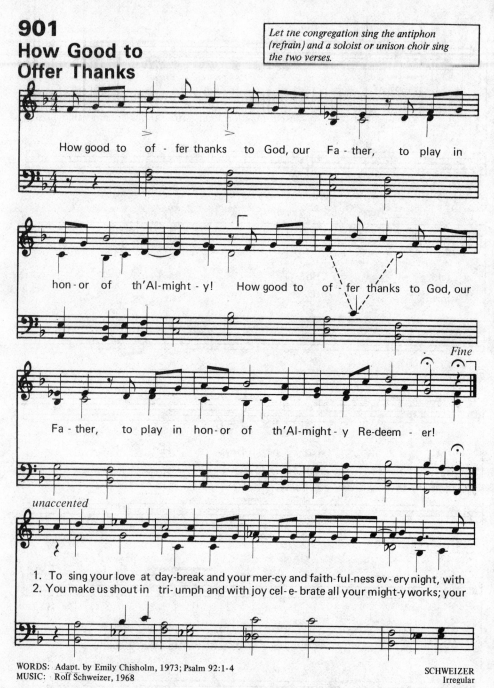

How good to of - fer thanks to God, our Fa - ther, to play in

hon - or of th'Al - might - y! How good to of - fer thanks to God, our

Fine

Fa - ther, to play in hon - or of th'Al - might - y Re - deem - er!

unaccented

1. To sing your love at day-break and your mer-cy and faith-ful-ness ev-ery night, with
2. You make us shout in tri-umph and with joy cel-e-brate all your might-y works; your

WORDS: Adapt. by Emily Chisholm, 1973; Psalm 92:1-4
MUSIC: Rolf Schweizer, 1968

SCHWEIZER
Irregular

Original title: Das ist ein köstlich Ding ©Copyright 1968 and English words ©Copyright 1973 by Hänssler-Verlag,
D-7303 Neuhausen-Stuttgart.

D.C. al Fine

ten-stringed lute and with zith - er, with mer - ry harp to praise you!
thoughts are past un - der-stand - ing, your deeds be - yond con - ceiv - ing!

902
Have You Got Good Religion?

Leader *(unaccompanied)*   Response   Leader
                                   G

1. Have you got good re - li - gion? Cer - t'nly, Lord! Have you

Response   Leader
D

got good re - li - gion? Cer - t'nly, Lord! Have you got good re - li - gion?

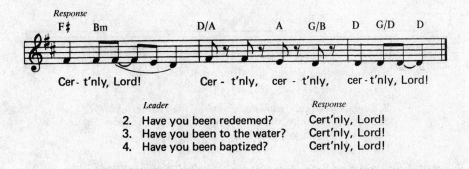

Response
F♯   Bm   D/A   A   G/B   D   G/D   D

Cer - t'nly, Lord!   Cer - t'nly, cer - t'nly, cer - t'nly, Lord!

Leader   Response
2. Have you been redeemed?   Cert'nly, Lord!
3. Have you been to the water? Cert'nly, Lord!
4. Have you been baptized?   Cert'nly, Lord!

WORDS and MUSIC: Trad. Negro Spiritual   CERTAINLY LORD

903
Hush, Hush, Somebody's Callin' Mah Name

Unison, unaccompanied. The "free" or added responses of (Hum) and (Thank you, Jesus) may be voiced by one or more singers to help set the mood and keep the rhythm.

Hush, hush, some-bod-y's call-in' mah name. Hush, hush,

some-bod-y's call-in' mah name, (yame, yame) Hush, hush, Some-bod-y's

call-in' mah name. O mah Lawd, O mah Lawd-ie, what shall I do?

Verse *

1. I'm so glad, trou-ble don't last al - ways. I'm so glad,

trou-ble don't last al - ways (yea, yea, yea). I'm so glad, trou-ble don't last al-

ways. O mah Lawd, O mah Lawd-ie, what shall I do?

* *Other stanzas may be added:*

2. Sounds like Jesus, somebody's callin' mah name., etc.
3. Soon one mornin', death'll come creepin' in mah room., etc.
4. I'm so glad, ah got mah religion in time., etc.
5. I'm so glad, I'm on mah journey home., etc.

WORDS: Trad. Negro Spiritual
MUSIC: Trad. harm. and notation by J. Jefferson Cleveland and Verolga Nix, 1979
Arr. copyright ©1979 by Abingdon.

HUSH
Irregular

I Come with Joy

1. I come with joy to meet my Lord, for - giv - en, loved, and free, In awe and won - der to re - call his life laid down for me, his life laid down for me.

2. I come with Chris - tians far and near to find, as all are fed, The new com - mu - ni - ty of love in Christ's com - mu - nion bread, in Christ's com - mu - nion bread.

3. As Christ breaks bread and bids us share each proud di - vi - sion ends. The love that made us makes us one, and stran - gers now are friends, and stran - gers now are friends.

4. And thus with joy we meet our Lord. His pres - ence al - ways near, Is in such friend - ship bet - ter known; we see and praise him here; we see and praise him here.

5. To - geth - er met, to - geth - er bound, we'll go our dif - ferent ways, And as his peo - ple in the world, we'll live and speak his praise, we'll live and speak his praise.

WORDS: Brian A. Wren, 1971
MUSIC: *Southern Harmony*, 1835; arr. by Austin C. Lovelace, 1977

DOVE OF PEACE
CM

905

I Danced in the Morning (Lord of the Dance)

The stanzas can be sung by designated small groups or by the choir, with everyone singing the refrain. Stanza 4 can be sung slowly and softly in minor.

In a strong two

1. I danced in the morn-ing when the world was be-gun, and I danced in the moon and the stars and the sun, And I came down from heav-en and I danced on the earth. At Beth-le-hem I had my birth.

2. I danced for the scribe and the phar-i-see, but they would not dance and they would not fol-low me; I danced for the fish-er-men, for James and John; they came to me and the dance went on.

3. I danced on the Sab-bath when I cured the lame, the ho-ly peo-ple said it was a shame; They whipped and they stripped and they hung me high; and they left me there on a cross to die.

4. I danced on a Fri-day and the sky turned black — it's hard to dance with the dev-il on your back; They bur-ied my bod-y and they thought I'd gone, but I am the dance and I still go on.

5. They cut me down and I leapt up high, I am the life that-'ll nev-er, nev-er die; I'll live in you if you'll live in me; I am the Lord of the Dance, said he.

WORDS: Sydney Carter, 1963
MUSIC: Adapt. from 19th cent. Shaker sources by Sydney Carter, 1963

LORD OF THE DANCE
Irregular

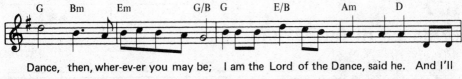

G   Bm   Em   G/B G   E/B   Am   D

Dance, then, wher-ev-er you may be; I am the Lord of the Dance, said he. And I'll

G   C   G   Bm   Am7   D7   G   C G

lead you all wher-ev-er you may   be, and I'll lead you all in the Dance, said he.

906
I Am the Church

Chorus

G   G/F♯   Em   D7

I am the church! You are the church! We are the church to - geth - er!

G   Em   Am   D   Bm   E   D7 G   *Fine*

All who fol-low Je-sus, all a-round the world! Yes, we're the church to-geth-er!

Verses G   C

1. The church is   not   a   build-ing,   the church is   not   a   stee - ple,   the
2. We're man – y   kinds of peo - ple   with man – y   kinds of   fac – es,   all
3. Some-times the church is march-ing,   some-times it's brave - ly   burn-ing,   some –
4. And when the   peo - ple gath - er   there's sing - ing and there's pray-ing,   there's
5. At   Pen - te - cost some peo - ple   re - ceived the Ho - ly   Spir - it   and
6. I   count if   I   am nine - ty,   or   nine or just   a   ba - by; there's

D   G   C6   D7   *D.C.*

church is   not   a   rest - ing place, the church   is   a   peo - ple!
col - ors and   all   ag - es, too, from   all   times and   plac - es.
times it's rid - ing,   some-times hid - ing,   al - ways   it's learn-ing:
laugh-ing and there's   cry - ing some-times,   all   of   it   say - ing:
told the Good News through the world to   all   who would hear   it.
one thing I   am   sure a - bout, and   I   don't mean may - be:

WORDS and MUSIC: Richard K. Avery and Donald S. Marsh, 1972

PORT JERVIS
Irregular

907
I Serve a Risen Savior

1. I serve a ris-en Sav-ior, he's in the world to-day; I
2. In all the world a-round me I see his lov-ing care, And
3. Re-joice, re-joice, O Chris-tian, lift up your voice and sing E-

know that he is liv-ing, what-ev-er some may say; I
though my heart grows wea-ry I nev-er will de-spair; I
ter-nal hal-le-lu-jahs to Je-sus Christ the King! The

see his hand of mer-cy, I hear his voice of cheer, And
know that he is lead-ing, through all the storm-y blast, The
hope of all who seek him, the help of all who find, None

just the time I need him he's al-ways near.
day of his ap-pear-ing will come at last.
oth-er is so lov-ing, so good and kind.

WORDS and MUSIC: Alfred H. Ackley, 1933 ; John 14:18-19

ACKLEY
76. 76. 76. 74.
with Refrain

He lives, he lives, Christ Je-sus lives to-day! He
He lives, he lives,

walks with me and talks with me a - long life's nar-row way. He

lives, he lives, sal - va - tion to im - part. You
He lives, he lives,

ask me how I know he lives? He lives with-in my heart!

908
I've Got Peace Like a River

I've got peace like a river, I've got peace like a river, I've got
I've got love like a river, I've got love like a river, I've got

peace like a riv-er in my soul.
love like a riv-er in my soul.
3. I've got joy like a

riv-er, I've got joy like a riv-er, I've got joy like a riv-er in my soul.

WORDS: Trad. Spiritual ; Isaiah 48:18
MUSIC: Trad., harm. by John Erickson

PEACE LIKE A RIVER
Irregular

909
I Wonder Why

I won-der why, I won-der why,

1. If his dis - ci - ples were like us here why they all
2. If they were peo - ple like you and me why they re -
3. If they were sol - diers like those we know why they all
4. If they were lead - ers like those we trust why they were
5. They did not know him and love him then: Would we al -

left him and ran in fear, As the world did cru - ci - fy,
fused then to set him free, For the crowd yelled: "Cru - ci - fy,"
beat him and mocked him so, Then went out to cru - ci - fy,
cru - el and so un - just When they judged to cru - ci - fy,
low him to die a - gain? Would the world still cru - ci - fy,

last time, repeat ad lib.

cru-ci-fy him? Oh, I won-der why. I won-der why. I won-der why.

WORDS and MUSIC: Richard K. Avery and Donald S. Marsh, 1970; Mark 15:20

WHY
Irregular

910
If You Have Ears

The dotted quarter equals 50 here, with the eighth note constant throughout. The hymn may be sung in unison, or it may be spoken while a keyboard instrument, preferably a piano, plays the accompaniment.

1. If you have ears, then lis - ten to what the Spir - it says and
3. If you have buds for tast - ing the ap - ple of God's eye, then
5. If you can smell the per - fume of life, the feast of earth, then

holding back

give an o - pen hear - ing to won - der and sur - prise.
go, en - joy cre - a - tion and peo - ple on the way.
sow the seeds of laugh - ter and tend the shoots of mirth.

a tempo

2. If you have eyes for hear - ing the word in hu - man form, then
4. If you have hands for car - ing, then pray that you may know the
6. Come, peo - ple, to your sen - ses and cel - e - brate the day! For

WORDS: Fred Kaan, 1967, 1971; Matthew 12:32 ; Matthew 13:16
MUSIC: Alec Wyton, 1977

LISTEN
13 13. 13 13.

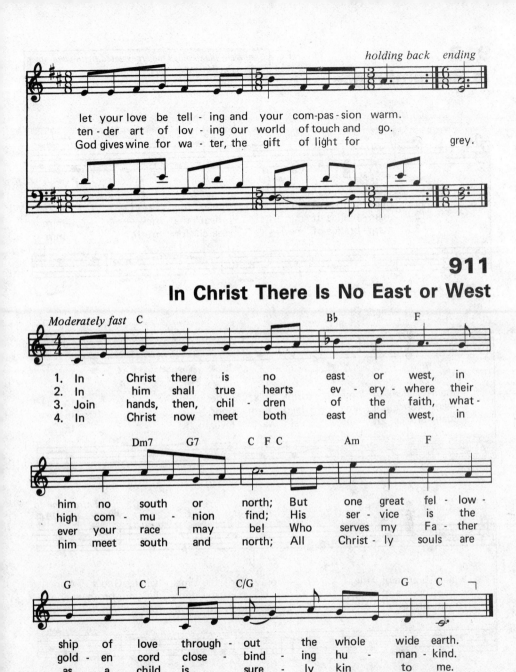

holding back *ending*

let your love be tell - ing and your com-pas-sion warm.
ten - der art of lov - ing our world of touch and go.
God gives wine for wa - ter, the gift of light for grey.

911
In Christ There Is No East or West

Moderately fast

1. In Christ there is no east or west, in
2. In him shall true hearts ev - ery - where their
3. Join hands, then, chil - dren of the faith, what -
4. In Christ now meet both east and west, in

him no south or north; But one great fel - low -
high com - mu - nion find; His ser - vice is the
ever your race may be! Who serves my Fa - ther
him meet south and north; All Christ - ly souls are

ship of love through - out the whole wide earth.
gold - en cord close - bind - ing hu - man - kind.
as a child is sure - ly kin to me.
one in him through - out the whole wide earth.

WORDS: John Oxenham, 1931; alt., Galatians 3:27-28
MUSIC: Afro-American Melody, adapt. by Harry T. Burleigh, 1939
Words used by permission of Desmond Dunkerley.

McKEE
CM

912
In Remembrance

Effective if piano plays the arpeggiated figures and organ the sustained chords.

In a gentle three

1. In re - mem - brance of me, eat this bread, In re -
(2.) mem - brance of me, heal the sick, In re -
(3.) mem - brance of me, search for truth, In re -

mem - brance of me, drink this wine. In re-
mem - brance of me, feed the poor. In re-
mem - brance of me, al - ways love. In re-

mem - brance of me, pray for the time when God's own
mem - brance of me, o - pen the door, let your broth - er and
mem - brance of me, don't look a - bove but in your

Third time to CODA

WORDS: Ragan Courtney, 1972 ; I Corinthians 11:24-25
MUSIC: Buryl Red, 1975

REMEMBRANCE
Irregular

(912-b)

bod- y and pre - cious blood shed for you, shed for you. 3. In re-

D. S. al CODA

CODA

heart look for God.

913
I Shall Not Be Moved

WORDS: Trad. Negro Spiritual
MUSIC: Trad. Negro Spiritual, arr. by J. Jefferson Cleveland and Verolga Nix, 1981.

Arr. copyright © 1981 by Abingdon.

ZION
Irregular

Additional verses 2. Jesus is my captain, I shall not be moved.
3. On my way to glory, I shall not be moved.
4. I'm climbing Jacob's ladder, I shall not be moved.
5. Old Satan tried to stop me, I shall not be moved.

914
Jesu, Jesu

In a gentle two
Refrain

Je - su, Je - su, fill us with your love, show

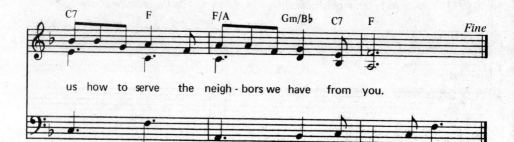

us how to serve the neigh - bors we have from you.

Fine

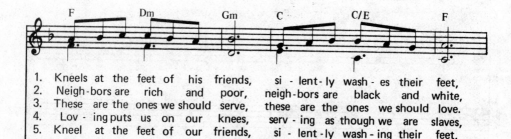

1. Kneels at the feet of his friends, si - lent - ly wash - es their feet,
2. Neigh-bors are rich and poor, neigh-bors are black and white,
3. These are the ones we should serve, these are the ones we should love.
4. Lov - ing puts us on our knees, serv - ing as though we are slaves,
5. Kneel at the feet of our friends, si - lent - ly wash - ing their feet,

WORDS: From Ghana, trans. by Tom Colvin; John 13: 3-5
MUSIC: Ghana Melody, arr. by Jane M. Marshall, 1981

CHEREPONI
Irregular

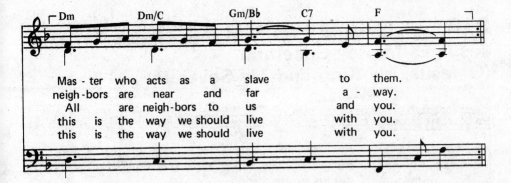

Master who acts as a slave to them.
neigh-bors are near and far a-way.
All are neigh-bors to us and you.
this is the way we should live with you.
this is the way we should live with you.

915
Joy Is Like the Rain (I Saw Raindrops)

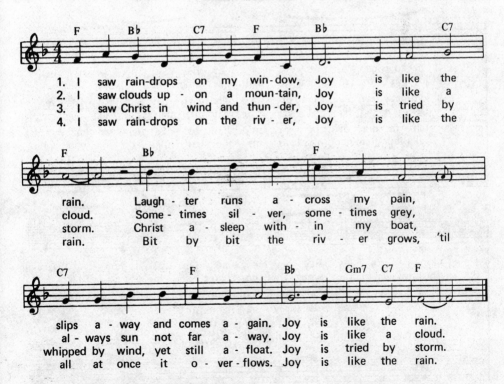

1. I saw rain-drops on my win-dow, Joy is like the
2. I saw clouds up-on a moun-tain, Joy is like a
3. I saw Christ in wind and thun-der, Joy is tried by
4. I saw rain-drops on the riv-er, Joy is like the

rain. Laugh-ter runs a-cross my pain,
cloud. Some-times sil-ver, some-times grey,
storm. Christ a-sleep with-in my boat,
rain. Bit by bit the riv-er grows, 'til

slips a-way and comes a-gain. Joy is like the rain.
al-ways sun not far a-way. Joy is like a cloud.
whipped by wind, yet still a-float. Joy is tried by storm.
all at once it o-ver-flows. Joy is like the rain.

WORDS and MUSIC: Sister Miriam Therese Winter

Words and music © MCMLXV by Medical Mission Sisters, Phil., Pa. Reprinted by permission Vanguard
Music Corp., 250 W. 57th Street, N.Y., N.Y. 10019. Further reproduction is prohibited. This song is
also available from Avant Garde Records at the same address.

JOY
8.5. 77.5.

916

Jesus Es Mi Rey Soberano
(O Jesus, My King and My Sovereign)

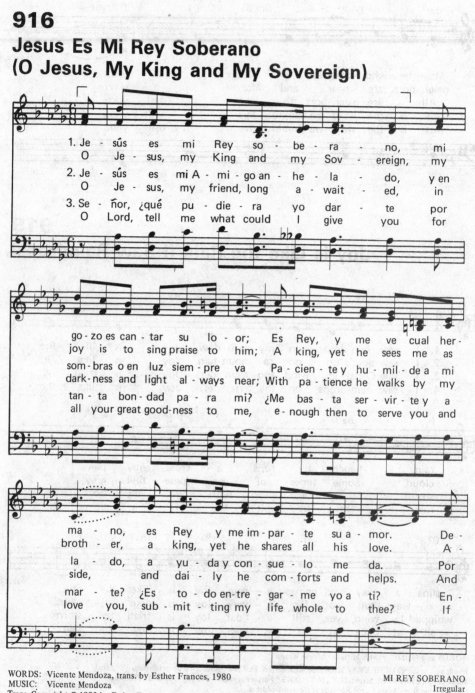

1. Je - sús es mi Rey so - be - ra - no, mi
   O Je - sus, my King and my Sov - ereign, my

2. Je - sús es mi A - mi - go an - he - la - do, y en
   O Je - sus, my friend, long a - wait - ed, in

3. Se - ñor, ¿qué pu - die - ra yo dar - te por
   O Lord, tell me what could I give you for

go - zo es can - tar su lo - or; Es Rey, y me ve cual her -
joy is to sing praise to him; A king, yet he sees me as

som - bras o en luz siem - pre va Pa - cien - te y hu - mil - de a mi
dark - ness and light al - ways near; With pa - tience he walks by my

tan - ta bon - dad pa - ra mi? ¿Me bas - ta ser - vir - te y a
all your great good - ness to me, e - nough then to serve you and

ma - no, es Rey y me im - par - te su a - mor. De -
broth - er, a king, yet he shares all his love. A -

la - do, a yu - da y con - sue - lo me da. Por
side, and dai - ly he com - forts and helps. And

mar - te? ¿Es to - do en - tre - gar - me yo a ti? En -
love you, sub - mit - ting my life whole to thee? If

WORDS: Vicente Mendoza, trans. by Esther Frances, 1980
MUSIC: Vicente Mendoza
Trans. Copyright © 1982 by Esther Frances. Used by permission.

MI REY SOBERANO
Irregular

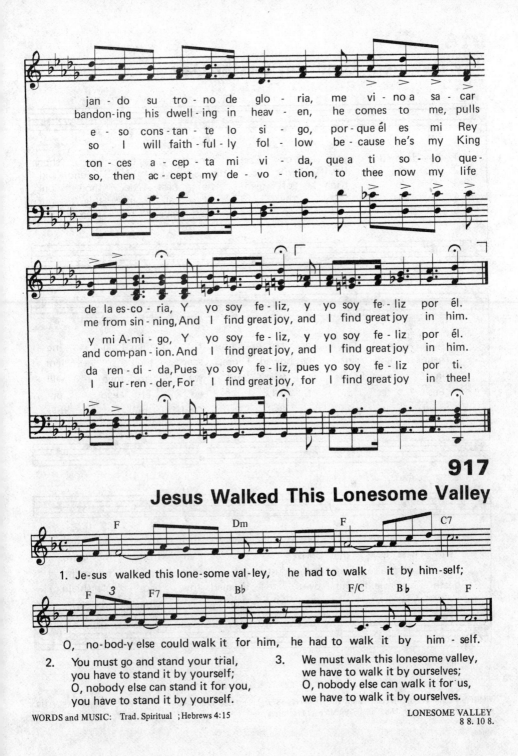

jan-do su tro-no de glo - ria, me vi-no a sa-car
bandon-ing his dwell-ing in heav - en, he comes to me, pulls

e - so cons-tan-te lo si - go, por-que él es mi Rey
so I will faith-ful-ly fol - low be-cause he's my King

ton-ces a-cep-ta mi vi - da, que a ti so-lo que-
so, then ac-cept my de-vo - tion, to thee now my life

de la es-co - ria, Y yo soy fe - liz, y yo soy fe-liz por él.
me from sin - ning, And I find great joy, and I find great joy in him.

y mi A-mi - go, Y yo soy fe - liz, y yo soy fe - liz por él.
and com-pan-ion. And I find great joy, and I find great joy in him.

da ren-di-da, Pues yo soy fe - liz, pues yo soy fe - liz por ti.
I sur-ren-der, For I find great joy, for I find great joy in thee!

917

Jesus Walked This Lonesome Valley

1. Je-sus walked this lone-some val-ley, he had to walk it by him-self;
O, no-bod-y else could walk it for him, he had to walk it by him-self.

2. You must go and stand your trial,
you have to stand it by yourself;
O, nobody else can stand it for you,
you have to stand it by yourself.

3. We must walk this lonesome valley,
we have to walk it by ourselves;
O, nobody else can walk it for us,
we have to walk it by ourselves.

WORDS and MUSIC: Trad. Spiritual ; Hebrews 4:15

LONESOME VALLEY
8 8. 10 8.

918
Joy Dawned Again on Easter Day

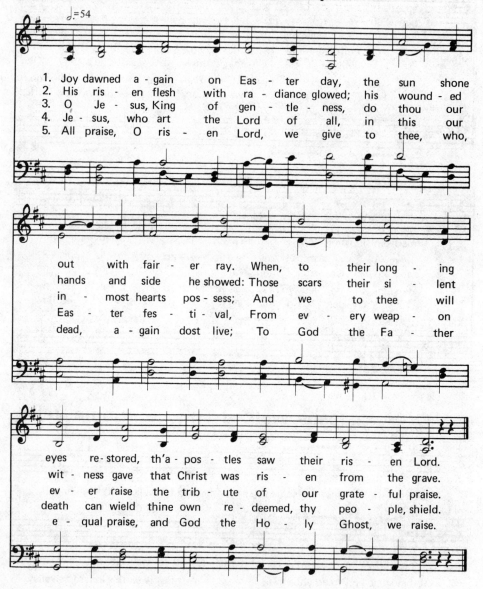

♩=54

1. Joy dawned a - gain on Eas - ter day, the sun shone
2. His ris - en flesh with ra - diance glowed; his wound - ed
3. O Je - sus, King of gen - tle - ness, do thou our
4. Je - sus, who art the Lord of all, in this our
5. All praise, O ris - en Lord, we give to thee, who,

out with fair - er ray. When, to their long - ing
hands and side he showed: Those scars their si - lent
in - most hearts pos - sess; And we to thee will
Eas - ter fes - ti - val, From ev - ery weap - on
dead, a - gain dost live; To God the Fa - ther

eyes re - stored, th'a - pos - tles saw their ris - en Lord.
wit - ness gave that Christ was ris - en from the grave.
ev - er raise the trib - ute of our grate - ful praise.
death can wield thine own re - deemed, thy peo - ple, shield.
e - qual praise, and God the Ho - ly Ghost, we raise.

WORDS: Anon. 4th or 5th cent.; trans. *The Hymnary*, 1872 ; Luke 24:36-39
MUSIC: *Piae Cantiones*, 1582; adapt. by Michael Praetorius

PUER NOBIS NASCITUR
LM

PUER NOBIS NASCITUR
Alternate Instrumental Accompaniment

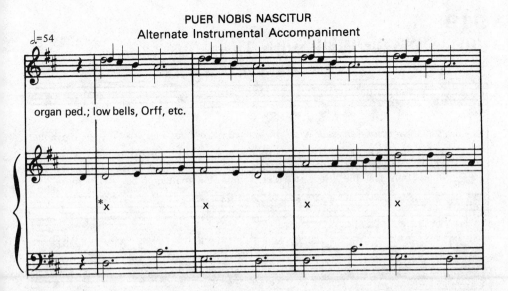

organ ped.; low bells, Orff, etc.

*finger cymbal *ad lib.* only

Alt. instr. acc. by John Erickson.

919
Just a Closer Walk with Thee

(Chorus) Just a clos-er walk with thee; grant it, Je-sus, if you please,
1. I am weak but thou art strong, Je-sus keep me from all wrong,
2. Through this world of toils and snares, if I fal-ter, Lord, who cares?
3. When my fee-ble life is o'er, time for me won't be no more.

Dai-ly walk-ing close with thee, let it be, dear Lord, let it be.
I'll be sat-is-fied as long as I walk, let me walk close with thee. (Chorus)
Who with me my bur-dens shares? None but thee, dear Lord, none but thee. (Chorus)
Guide me gent-ly, safe-ly o'er to thy king-dom shore, to thy shore. (Chorus)

WORDS: Trad.
MUSIC: Trad., arr. by John Erickson, 1981
Arr. copyright © 1982 by John Erickson. Used by permission.

CLOSER WALK
77. 78.

920
I Wish I Could Sing
(Könnte Singen Ich)

Two measures of drumbeat or hand claps can introduce this African spiritual (but drop out at the "Hosannas.") Let the eighth note remain constant throughout.

I wish I could sing as an-gels can sing. I wish I could fly as
Könnte sing-en ich wie En-gel so schön. Könnte flie-gen ich wie

an-gels can fly! I'd like to soar with heav-en-ly wings like oth-er
En-gel so schön! Sing-end auf-schwing-en nür-de ich mich, bring-en dem

WORDS and MUSIC: Zaire Congolese Spiritual, trans. and arr. by Ruby Wiebe
Copyright © 1978 by Mennonite World Conference, Lombard, IL. Used by permission.

ZAIRE
Irregular

an - gels, then I'd sing a heav-en-ly song, I'd sing all day long.
Schöp- fer ganz innig-lich ein nue - es Lied, ein lieb - lich - es Lied.

High voices
sing praise to God!
Lob - preis - et Gott!

sing praise to God!
Lob - preis - et Gott!

Low voices Hal - le - lu - jah,

Hal - le - lu - jah,

sing praise to God!
Lob - preis - et Gott!

D. C. al Fine

Hal - le - lu - jah,

All
Ho - san - na, ho - san - na!
Ho - sian - na, ho - sian - na!

Drum Beat:

921
Kum Ba Yah

1. Kum ba yah, my Lord, kum ba yah! Kum ba yah, my Lord,
2. Some-one's cry - ing, Lord, kum ba yah! Some-one's cry - ing, Lord,
3. Some-one's sing - ing, Lord, kum ba yah! Some-one's sing - ing, Lord,
4. Some-one's pray - ing, Lord, kum ba yah! Some-one's pray - ing, Lord,

kum ba yah! Kum ba yah, my Lord, kum ba yah! O Lord, kum ba yah!
kum ba yah! Some-one's cry - ing, Lord, kum ba yah! O Lord, kum ba yah!
kum ba yah! Some-one's sing-ing, Lord, kum ba yah! O Lord, kum ba yah!
kum ba yah! Some-one's pray-ing, Lord, kum ba yah! O Lord, kum ba yah!

WORDS and MUSIC: Traditional

KUM BA YAH
Irregular

922
Lift High the Cross

Unison ♩ = 88

Lift high the cross, the love of Christ pro - claim

(Fine)

till all the world a - dore his sa - cred name.

Harmony

1. Come, Chris - tians, fol - low where our Cap - tain trod,
2. Led on their way by this tri - um - phant sign,
3. Each new - born sol - dier of the Cru - ci - fied
4. O Lord, once lift - ed on the glo - rious tree,
5. So shall our song of tri - umph ev - er be:

D. C. al Fine

our King vic - to - rious, Christ, the Son of God.
the hosts of God in - con-quering ranks com - bine.
bears on his brow the seal of him who died.
as thou hast prom - ised, draw us un - to thee.
praise to the Cru - ci - fied for vic - to - ry!

WORDS: George William Kitchin and Michael Robert Newbolt, 1916 ; I Corinthians 1:18
MUSIC: Sydney Hugo Nicholson, 1916

CRUCIFER
10 10. 10. 10.

Words, music, and setting by permission of *Hymns Ancient and Modern*

Like Survivors of the Flood

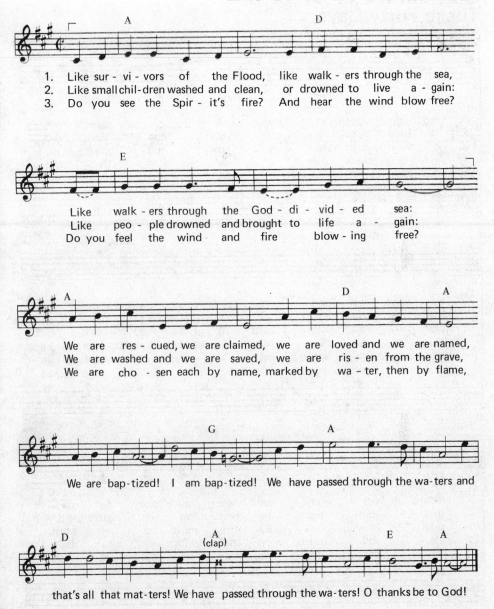

1. Like sur - vi - vors of the Flood, like walk - ers through the sea,
2. Like small chil - dren washed and clean, or drowned to live a - gain:
3. Do you see the Spir - it's fire? And hear the wind blow free?

Like walk - ers through the God - di - vid - ed sea:
Like peo - ple drowned and brought to life a - gain:
Do you feel the wind and fire blow - ing free?

We are res - cued, we are claimed, we are loved and we are named,
We are washed and we are saved, we are ris - en from the grave,
We are cho - sen each by name, marked by wa - ter, then by flame,

We are bap - tized! I am bap - tized! We have passed through the wa - ters and

(clap)

that's all that mat - ters! We have passed through the wa - ters! O thanks be to God!

WORDS and MUSIC: Richard K. Avery and Donald S. Marsh, 1971 ; Romans 6:3-4

BAPTIZED
Irregular

924
Lord, Who Throughout
These Forty Days

1. Lord, who through-out these for - ty days for
2. As thou with Sa - tan didst con - tend, and
3. As thou didst hun - ger bear and thirst, so
4. And through these days of pen - i - tence, and
5. A - bide with us, that so, this life of

us didst fast and pray, Teach us with thee to
didst the vic - tory win, O give us strength in
teach us, gra - cious Lord, To die to self, and
through thy Pas - sion tide, Yea, ev - er - more in
suf - fering o - ver - past, An Eas - ter of un -

mourn our sins, and close by thee to stay.
thee to fight, In thee to con - quer sin.
chief - ly live, By thy most ho - ly word.
life and death, Je - sus! with us a - bide.
end - ing joy We may at - tain at last.

WORDS: Claudia F. Hernaman, 1873; Matthew 4:1-2
MUSIC: *Supplement to Kentucky Harmony,* 1820, harm. by Austin C. Lovelace, 1964

DETROIT
CM

Treble

1. Lord, who through-out these for - ty days for

Melody

2. As thou with Sa - tan didst con - tend, and

Bass

3. As thou didst hun - ger bear and thirst, so

us didst fast and pray, Teach us with thee to

didst the vic - tory win, O give us strength in

teach us, gra - cious Lord, To die to self, and

(924-b)

mourn our sins, and close by thee to stay.

thee to fight, In thee to con - quer sin.

chief - ly live, By thy most ho - ly word.

925
Lord, We Praise You

| G | C | A7 | D | D7 |

1. Lord, we praise you, Lord, we praise you,

| G | G7 | C | G/D | D7 | G |

Lord, we praise you, we praise you, Lord!

2. Lord, we thank . . .   3. Lord, we love . . .

WORDS and MUSIC: Otis Skillings, 1972

SHULL
44. 44.

926
Lovely Child, Holy Child

1. Love - ly Child, ho - ly Child, gen - tle, mild, un - de - filed;
2. Child of light, born to - night, our de - light, prom - ise bright;
3. Rest thy head, sweet - est head; gifts we'll spread at thy bed.
4. To this Boy, our great joy, we em - ploy hymns of joy;

In - fant King, fair - est King, gifts we'll bring and an - thems sing:
Child so fair: see him there; now de - clare him ev - ery - where:
Je - sus Lord, be a - dored, may this word now be out - poured:
Child so fair: see him there; now de - clare him ev - ery - where:

Al - le - lu - ia, al - le - lu - ia.

Al - le - lu - ia, al - le - lu - ia!

WORDS: David N. Johnson, 1968; Matthew 2:11
MUSIC: Folk Carol, adapt. by David N. Johnson, 1968

BETHLEHEM
66.67. with Alleluias

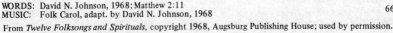

927

Lord, Let Me Love

In an easy two

1. Lord, let me love; let lov-ing be the sym-bol of
2. Lord, let me love, though love may be the los-ing of
3. Lord, let me love the low-ly and the hum-ble, for-let
4. Lord, let my par-ish be the world un-bound-ed, let

grace that warms my heart; and let me find
ev-ery earth-ly trea-sure I pos-sess.
get-ting not the might-y and the strong;
love of race and clan be at an end;

Thy lov-ing hand to still me when I trem-ble at
Lord, make thy love the pat-tern of my choos-ing, and
And give me grace to love those who may stum-ble, nor
Let ev-ery hate-ful doc-trine be con-found-ed that

WORDS: C. Eric Lincoln, c. 1958
MUSIC: Carlton Young, 1982

LINCOLN
11 10. 11 10.

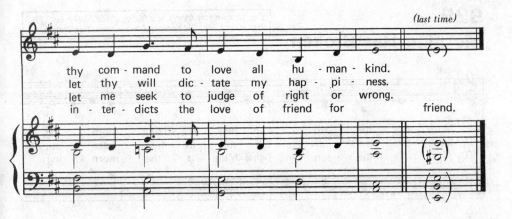

thy com - mand to love all hu - man - kind.
let thy will dic - tate my hap - pi - ness.
let me seek to judge of right or wrong.
in - ter - dicts the love of friend for friend.

(last time)

928
May the Lord, Mighty God

May the Lord, might - y God, bless and keep you for - ev - er;

Fine

Grant you peace, per - fect peace, cour - age in ev - ery en - deav - or.

Voice I

Lift up your eyes and see his face and his grace for - ev - er;

Voice II

Lift up and see his face, his grace for - ev - er;

D.C.

May the Lord, might - y God, bless and keep you for - ev - er.

D.C.

May the Lord, might - y God, bless and keep you for - ev - er.

WORDS: Anon. , Psalm 29:11
MUSIC: Chinese Folk Song, probably by Pao-chen Li c. 1960

WEN-TI
Irregular

929
Morning Has Broken

Sing this unison hymn in a lilting three-to-the-bar. The first stanza may be repeated as a concluding stanza.

Unison

1. Morn - ing has bro - ken like the first morn - ing,
2. Sweet the rain's new fall sun lit from heav - en,
3. Mine is the sun - light! Mine is the morn - ing

Black-bird has spo - ken like the first bird.
Like the first dew - fall on the first grass.
Born of the one light E - den saw play!

Praise for the sing - ing! Praise for the morn - ing!
Praise for the sweet - ness of the wet gar - den,
Praise with e - la - tion, praise ev - ery morn - ing,

Praise for them, spring - ing fresh from the Word!
Sprung in com - plete - ness where his feet pass.
God's re - cre - a - tion of the new day!

WORDS: Eleanor Farjeon, 1931 ; II Peter 1:19
MUSIC: Traditional Gaelic Melody, harm. by David Evans, 1927

BUNESSAN
10 9. 10 9.

Words copyrighted; used by permission of David Higham Associates, Ltd., London.
Music from the *Revised Church Hymnary*, 1927. Used by permission of Oxford University Press.

This is effective when sung by a soloist or the choir, with the congregation echoing the end of each phrase and joining in on the refrain.

My Lord Came Walking Over the Sea

1. My Lord came walk - ing o - ver the sea,
2. My Lord came call - ing o - ver the sea,
3. My Lord, I'm fall - ing in - to the sea,
4. Be - lieve, my dear one, o - ver the sea,

My Lord came walk - ing o - ver to me:
My Lord came call - ing o - ver to me:
My Lord, I'm fall - ing, come res-cue me:
Be - lieve, my dear one, on - ly in me:

Refrain

The waves are high, the winds are strong: Sing me, Lord, your walk-ing song.

WORDS: Hamish Swanston : Matthew 14:25,29-30
MUSIC: Elizabeth Poston, 1971
Reprinted from *The New Catholic Hymnal* by permission of the publisher, Faber Music Ltd., London.

ST. PETER'S SONG
5 4.5 4.with Refrain

931
My Soul Gives Glory (Magnificat)

1. My soul gives glo - ry to the Lord, in God my Sav - ior
2. His mer - cy goes to all who fear, from age to age and
3. He raised his ser - vant Is - ra - el, re - mem-bering his e -

I re - joice. My low - li - ness he did re - gard, ex - alt - ing
to all parts. His arm of strength to all is near; he scat - ters
ter - nal grace, As from of old he did fore - tell to A - bra -

me by his own choice. From this day all shall call me blest,
those who have proud hearts. He casts the might - y from their throne
ham and all his race. O Fa - ther, Son, and Spir - it blest,

for he has done great things for me. Of all great names his
and rais - es those of low de - gree; He feeds the hun - gry
in three - fold Name are you a - dored. To you be ev - ery

WORDS: Luke 1:46-55; trans. by J. T. Mueller, 1940, alt.
MUSIC: Michael Joncas, 1979

MARY'S CANTICLE
LMD

is   the   best,   for   it   is   ho - ly,   strong   is   he.
as   his   own,   the   rich   de - part   in   pov - er - ty.
prayer ad - dressed, from   age   to   age   the   on - ly   Lord.

932
Now Let Us from This Table Rise

1. Now   let   us   from   this   ta - ble   rise   re - newed   in
2. With   minds   a - lert,   up - held   by   grace,   to   spread   the
3. To   fill   each   hu - man   house   with   love,   it   is   the
4. Then   grant   us   cour - age,   Fa - ther   God,   to   choose   a -

bod - y,   mind,   and   soul;   With   Christ   we   die   and
Word   in   speech   and   deed,   We   fol - low   in   the
sac - ra - ment   of   care;   The   work   that   Christ   be -
gain   the   pil - grim   way   And   help   us   to   ac -

live   a - gain,   his   self - less   love   has   made   us   whole.
steps   of   Christ,   at   one   with   us   in   hope   and   need.
gan   to   do   we   hum - bly   pledge   our - selves   to   share.
cept   with   joy   the   chal - lenge   of   to - mor - row's   day.

WORDS: Fred Kaan, 1968
MUSIC: *Grenoble Antiphoner*, 1753

DEUS TUORUM MILITUM
LM

933
Nothing Between

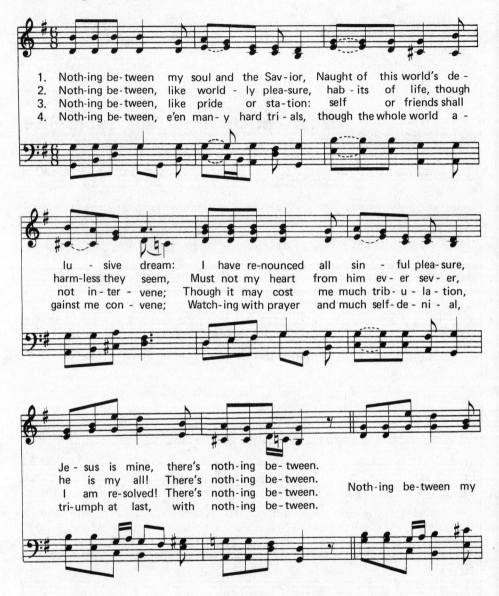

1. Nothing between my soul and the Savior, Naught of this world's de-
2. Nothing between, like worldly pleasure, habits of life, though
3. Nothing between, like pride or station: self or friends shall
4. Nothing between, e'en many hard trials, though the whole world a-

lusive dream: I have renounced all sinful pleasure,
harmless they seem, Must not my heart from him ever sever,
not intervene; Though it may cost me much tribulation,
gainst me convene; Watching with prayer and much self-denial,

Jesus is mine, there's nothing between.
he is my all! There's nothing between.
I am resolved! There's nothing between.
triumph at last, with nothing between.

Nothing between my

WORDS and MUSIC: Charles A. Tindley; arr. by J. Edward Hoy, 1979
Arr. copyright ©1979

TINDLEY
Irregular with Refrain

soul and the Sav-ior, so that his bless - ed face may be seen; Noth-ing pre-

vent-ing the least of his fa-vor: keep the way clear! Let noth-ing be-tween.

934
O Lamb of God (Agnus Dei)

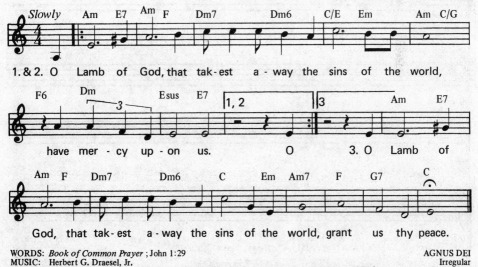

Slowly Am E7 Am F Dm7 Dm6 C/E Em Am C/G

1. & 2. O   Lamb of God, that tak-est   a - way   the   sins   of   the   world,

F6 Dm Esus E7 |1, 2 |3 Am E7

have mer - cy up - on us. O 3. O Lamb of

Am F Dm7 Dm6 C Em Am7 F G7 C

God, that tak-est a - way the sins of the world, grant us thy peace.

WORDS: *Book of Common Prayer*; John 1:29
MUSIC: Herbert G. Draesel, Jr.

AGNUS DEI
Irregular

935
O God, Who Dwells in Light Above

1. O God, who dwells in light a - bove, yet looks up - on us with thy love,
2. Re - vive our will, re - new our nerve, that as we leave this place to serve

Now keep us stead - fast as we part, re - freshed in mind and soul and heart.
In of - fice, school - room, church, or home, we bring thy peace, sha - lom, sha - lom.

Descant

3. Praise God, from whom all bless - ings flow, praise him, all crea - tures

Melody

here be - low, Praise him a - bove, ye heaven - ly host, praise

Fa - ther, Son, and Ho - ly Ghost. A - men.

WORDS: Jane Marshall, 1976; St. 3, Thomas Ken, 1637-1711
MUSIC: Thomas Tallis, *The Whole Psalter*, 1561-67; descant, Jane Marshall, 1976

TALLIS' CANON
LM

O Jesus Christ, to You May Hymns

1. O Je-sus Christ, to you may hymns be ris - ing
2. Show us your Spir - it, brood-ing o'er each cit - y,
3. Grant us new cour - age, sac - ri - fi - cial, hum - ble,

in ev - ery cit - y for your love and care;
as you once wept a - bove Je - ru - sa - lem,
strong in your strength to ven - ture and to dare;

In - spire our wor - ship, grant the glad sur - pris - ing
Seek - ing to gath - er all in love and pit - y,
To lift the fall - en, guide the feet that stum - ble,

that your blest Spir - it brings us ev - ery - where.
and heal - ing those who touch your gar - ment's hem.
seek out the lone - ly and God's mer - cy share.

WORDS: Bradford Webster, 1954
MUSIC: Daniel Moe, 1957

CITY OF GOD
11 10. 11 10.

937
O Love, How Deep

1. O love, how deep, how broad, how high,
2. For us baptized, for us he bore
3. For us he prayed; for us he taught;

be - yond all thought and fan - ta - sy,
his ho - ly fast and hun - gered sore;
for us his dai - ly works he wrought,

That God, the Son of God, should take
For us temp - ta - tion sharp he knew;
By words and signs and ac - tions thus

our mor - tal form for mor - tals' sake!
for us the temp - ter o - ver - threw.
still seek - ing not him - self, but us.

WORDS: Latin 15th cent.; trans. by Benjamin Webb, *The Hymnal Noted*, Part II 1854 ; John 15:13
MUSIC: English Melody, 15th cent.

DEO GRACIAS

O the Shame

As a musical version of the Prodigal Son parable, this can be effectively used as a solo with string quartet accompaniment.

1. O the shame that fills my heart, O the deep re-morse,
   Fol-low-ing vain and emp-ty dreams, soon to fade a-way,

2. Liv-ing in a grass-y hut, feed-ing hun-gry swine,
   Stom-ach emp-ty, bod-y cold, can this real-ly be?

3. See my torn and tat-tered clothes, they are drenched with dew.
   I am go-ing home at once, fa-ther's par-don plead.

Since I left my fa-ther's house, took my will-ful course.
Tast-ing fick-le hap-pi-ness here for but a day.

Un-ac-cus-tomed to the work that must needs be mine.
O how thin a cloak it is! hu-man sym-pa-thy.

It's high time to come a-wake; with this dream I'm through!
Sure-ly he will take me in when he knows my need.

WORDS: Sogo Matsumoto, trans. by J. A. McAlpine; Luke 15:11-19
MUSIC: Trad. Japanese Melody, arr. by Kaza Nakaseko, 1963

IMAYO
75. 75. D.

Alternate Accompaniment

MUSIC: Trad. Japanese Melody harm. by Isao Koizumi, 1954

IMAYO
75. 75. D.

939
On Christmas Night

1. On Christ-mas night all Chris-tians sing to hear the news the an - gels bring. On Christ-mas night all Chris-tians sing to hear the news the an - gels bring — News of great joy, news of great mirth, news of our mer - ci - ful King's birth.

2. Then why should we on earth be so sad, since our Re-deem - er made us glad? Then why should we on earth be so sad, since our Re-deem - er made us glad, When from our sin he set us free, all for to gain our lib - er - ty?

4. All out of dark - ness we have light, which made the an - gels sing this night. All out of dark - ness we have light, which made the an - gels sing this night: "Glo - ry to God and peace to men, now and for ev - er - more. A - men."

WORDS: Traditional; Luke 2:10-11
MUSIC: Trad. English Carol; arr. by Ralph Vaughan Williams, 1919

SUSSEX CAROL
88. 88. 88.

940
O Welcome All

1. O wel-come all you no-ble saints of old,
2. Who is this who spreads the vic-tory feast?
3. Beg-gars, lame, and har-lots al-so here;
4. Wor-ship in the pres-ence of the Lord,

as now be-fore your ver-y eyes un-fold
Who is this who makes our war-ring cease?
re-pen-tant pub-li-cans are draw-ing near;
with joy-ful songs and hearts in one ac-cord,

the won-ders all so long a-go fore-told.
Je-sus, Ris-en Sav-ior, Prince of Peace.
way-ward ones come home with-out a fear.
and let our Host at ta-ble be a-dored.

God and man at ta-ble are sat down.
(God, with all, at ta-ble is sat down.)

God and man at ta-ble are sat down.
(God, with all, at ta-ble is sat down.)

WORDS and MUSIC: Robert J. Stamps, 1972 ; Luke 14:15-24
Copyright © 1972 by Robert J. Stamps. Used by permission.

CENÉDIUS
Irregular

On Jordan's Banks the Baptist's Cry

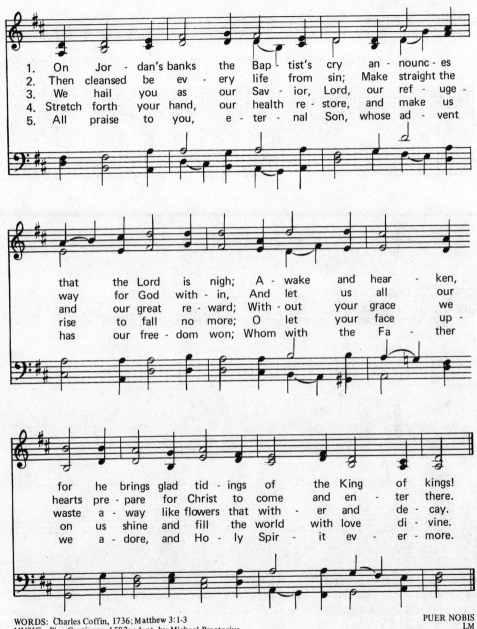

1. On Jor - dan's banks the Bap - tist's cry an - nounc - es
2. Then cleansed be ev - ery life from sin; Make straight the
3. We hail you as our Sav - ior, Lord, our ref - uge
4. Stretch forth your hand, our health re - store, and make us
5. All praise to you, e - ter - nal Son, whose ad - vent

that the Lord is nigh; A - wake and hear - ken,
way for God with - in, And let us all our
and our great re - ward; With - out your grace we
rise to fall no more; O let your face up -
has our free - dom won; Whom with the Fa - ther

for he brings glad tid - ings of the King of kings!
hearts pre - pare for Christ to come and en - ter there.
waste a - way like flowers that with - er and de - cay.
on us shine and fill the world with love di - vine.
we a - dore, and Ho - ly Spir - it ev - er - more.

WORDS: Charles Coffin, 1736; Matthew 3:1-3
MUSIC: *Piae Cantiones*, 1582; adapt. by Michael Praetorius

PUER NOBIS
LM

942
Our Father

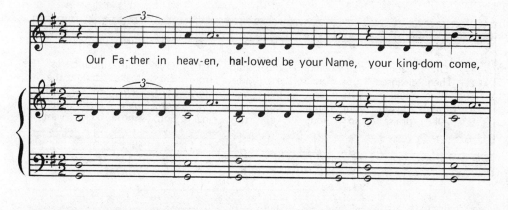

Our Fa-ther in heav-en, hal-lowed be your Name, your king-dom come,

your will be done on earth as in heav-en. Give us to-

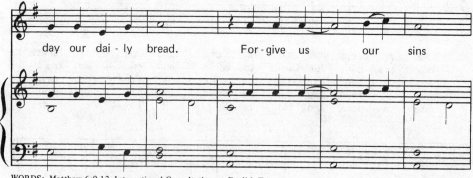

day our dai-ly bread. For-give us our sins

WORDS: Matthew 6:9-13; International Consultation on English Texts
MUSIC: John Erickson, 1977

Music copyright © 1982 by John Erickson. Used by permission.

LORD'S PRAYER
Irregular

943
O Wondrous Type! O Vision Fair

Unison

1. O won - drous type! O vi - sion fair of
2. With Mo - ses and E - li - jah nigh the in -
3. With shin - ing face and bright ar - ray, Christ
4. And faith - ful hearts are raised on high by
5. O Fa - ther, with the e - ter - nal Son and

glo - ry that the church may share, Which
car - nate Lord holds con - verse high; And
deigns to man - i - fest to - day What
this great vi - sion's mys - ter - y; For
Ho - ly Spir - it ev - er one, We

Christ up - on the moun - tain shows where
from the cloud the Ho - ly One bears
glo - ry shall be theirs a - bove who
which in joy - ful strains we raise the
pray you, bring us by your grace to

WORDS: *Sarum*, 15th cent.; trans. by John M. Neale, 1854, alt.; Matthew 17:1-3
MUSIC: English, 15th cent.

DEO GRACIAS
LM

bright - er than the sun he glows!
rec - ord to the on - ly Son.
joy in God with per - fect love.
voice of prayer, the hymn of praise.
see your glo - ry face to face.

944
O the Lamb

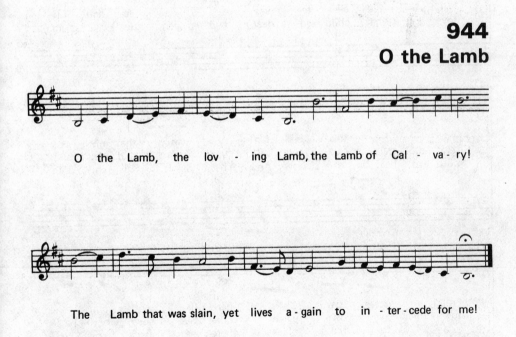

O the Lamb, the lov - ing Lamb, the Lamb of Cal - va - ry!

The Lamb that was slain, yet lives a - gain to in - ter - cede for me!

WORDS and MUSIC: 19th cent. American camp meeting; from *The Revivalist*, 1872; Revelation 5:12   THE LAMB
                arr. by Ellen Jane Lorenz   Irregular
Adaptation copyright © 1982 by Ellen Jane Lorenz. Used by permission.

945
Once in Royal David's City

1. Once in roy-al Da-vid's cit-y stood a low-ly cat-tle shed, Where a moth-er laid her ba-by in a man-ger for his bed: Ma-ry was that moth-er mild, Je-sus Christ, her lit-tle child.

2. He came down to earth from heav-en who is God and Lord of all, And his shel-ter was a sta-ble, and his cra-dle was a stall: With the poor and mean and low-ly lived on earth our Sav-ior ho-ly.

3. And our eyes at last shall see him, through his own re-deem-ing love; For that child so dear and gen-tle is our Lord in heav-en a-bove, And he leads his chil-dren on to the place where he is gone.

WORDS: Cecil Francis Alexander, 1848; Luke 2:7
MUSIC: Henry John Gauntlett, 1849

IRBY
87. 87. 87.

Praise and Thanksgiving Be to God

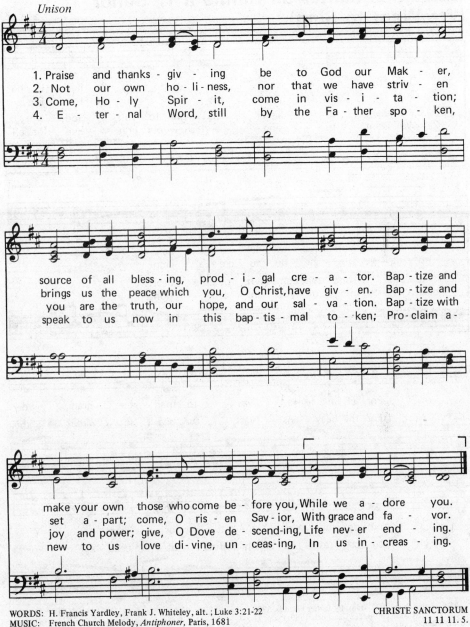

Unison

1. Praise and thanks-giv-ing be to God our Mak-er,
2. Not our own ho-li-ness, nor that we have striv-en
3. Come, Ho-ly Spir-it, come in vis-i-ta-tion;
4. E-ter-nal Word, still by the Fa-ther spo-ken,

source of all bless-ing, prod-i-gal cre-a-tor. Bap-tize and
brings us the peace which you, O Christ, have giv-en. Bap-tize and
you are the truth, our hope, and our sal-va-tion. Bap-tize with
speak to us now in this bap-tis-mal to-ken; Pro-claim a-

make your own those who come be-fore you, While we a-dore you.
set a-part; come, O ris-en Sav-ior, With grace and fa-vor.
joy and power; give, O Dove de-scend-ing, Life nev-er end-ing.
new to us love di-vine, un-ceas-ing, In us in-creas-ing.

WORDS: H. Francis Yardley, Frank J. Whiteley, alt.; Luke 3:21-22
MUSIC: French Church Melody, *Antiphoner*, Paris, 1681
Text used by permission of H. Francis Yardley.

CHRISTE SANCTORUM
11 11 11. 5.

947

Queremos Cantar un Himno a Ti, Señor
(We Want to Sing)

1. Que-re-mos can-tar, un him-no_a ti, Se-ñor U-na
2. Que-re-mos can-tar, y gra-ti-tud mos-trar Por

1. We want to sing a hymn to you, O God, a
2. We want to sing and show our grat-i-tude for all

nue-va can-ción que es del co-ra-zón.
to-da be-lle-za de tu cre-a-ción.

new song that comes out of the heart.
beau-ti-ful things of your cre-a-tion.

Por el cie-lo vas-to, mar tan gran-de de
For the heav-ens vast, the sea so great, the

Y_el mun-do be-llo que tu for-mas-te, Y
world you cre-at-ed in forms of beau-ty, For

WORDS: Luiza Cruz, 1972; trans. by Esther Frances, 1980,
    alt. by John and Roger Deschner, 1980; Psalm 33:3-7
MUSIC: Luiza Cruz, 1972

QUEREMOS CANTAR
Irregular

Trans. copyright © 1980 by Esther Frances. Used by permission. Alt. of text copyright © 1982 by John
and Roger Deschner. Used by permission.

948
Peace I Leave You

Peace I leave you, peace I leave you, go now and spread the word,

Tell the good news you've heard: God lives in love.

WORDS: Traditional ; John 14:27
MUSIC: Israeli Melody

PEACE
Irregular

Permission granted by Choristers Guild, P.O. Box 38188, Dallas, TX 75238.

949
Rejoice in the Lord
Round

Re-joice in the Lord al - ways, and a - gain I say Re - joice!

Re-joice in the Lord al - ways, and a - gain I say Re - joice!

Re - joice! Re - joice! And a - gain I say Re - joice!

Re - joice! Re - joice! And a - gain I say Re - joice!

WORDS: Philippians 4:4-9
MUSIC: Traditional

REJOICE
Irregular

Rejoice, Ye Pure in Heart

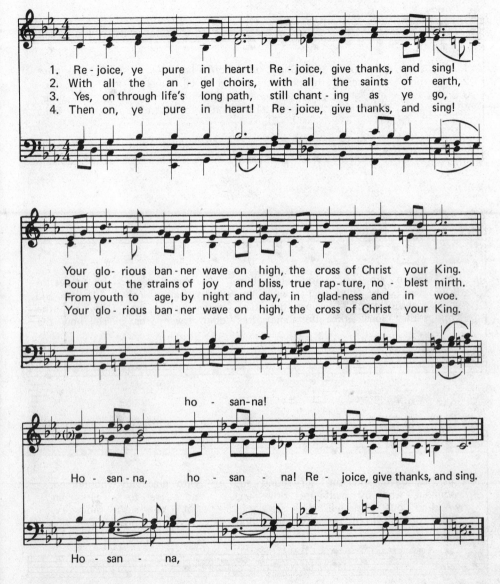

1. Re - joice, ye pure in heart! Re - joice, give thanks, and sing!
2. With all the an - gel choirs, with all the saints of earth,
3. Yes, on through life's long path, still chant - ing as ye go,
4. Then on, ye pure in heart! Re - joice, give thanks, and sing!

Your glo - rious ban - ner wave on high, the cross of Christ your King.
Pour out the strains of joy and bliss, true rap - ture, no - blest mirth.
From youth to age, by night and day, in glad - ness and in woe.
Your glo - rious ban - ner wave on high, the cross of Christ your King.

ho - san - na!

Ho - san - na, ho - san - na! Re - joice, give thanks, and sing.

Ho - san - na,

WORDS: Edward H. Plumptre, 1865; Philippians 4:4
MUSIC: Richard Dirksen, 1974

VINEYARD HAVEN
SM with Refrain

951
Rise, Shine, You People

Unison

1. Rise, shine, you peo - ple! Christ the Lord has en - tered our
2. See how he sends the powers of e - vil reel - ing; he
3. Come, cel - e - brate; your ban - ners high un - furl - ing; your
4. Tell how the Fa - ther sent his Son to save us. Tell

hu - man sto - ry; God in him is cen - tered. He comes to
brings us free - dom, light and life and heal - ing. All men and
songs and prayers a - gainst the dark - ness hurl - ing. To all the
of the Son, who life and free - dom gave us. Tell how the

us, by death and sin sur - round - ed, with grace un - bound - ed.
wom - en, who by guilt are driv - en, now are for - giv - en.
world go out and tell the sto - ry of Je - sus' glo - ry.
Spir - it calls from ev - ery na - tion his new cre - a - tion.

WORDS: Ronald A. Klug, 1973 ; Isaiah 60:1
MUSIC: Dale Wood, 1973

WOJTKIEWIECZ
11 11. 11 5.

952
Seek Ye First

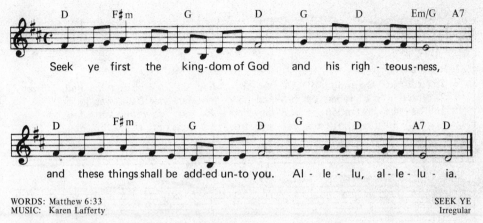

Seek ye first the king-dom of God and his righ-teous-ness,

and these things shall be add-ed un-to you. Al - le - lu, al - le - lu - ia.

WORDS: Matthew 6:33
MUSIC: Karen Lafferty

SEEK YE
Irregular

953
Shalom
(Fare Well, Dear Friends)

Round

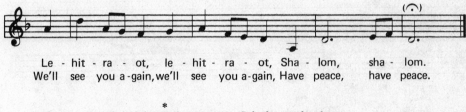

Sha - lom cha - ve - rim, sha - lom cha - ve - rim. Sha - lom, sha - lom.
Fare well, dear friends, stay safe, dear friends, Have peace, have peace.

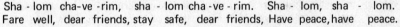
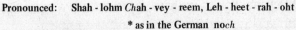

Le - hit - ra - ot, le - hit - ra - ot, Sha - lom, sha - lom.
We'll see you a - gain, we'll see you a - gain, Have peace, have peace.

*
Pronounced: Shah - lohm *Ch*ah - vey - reem, Leh - heet - rah - oht

* as in the German no*ch*

WORDS: Trans. from Hebrew and adapt. by Roger N. Deschner, 1980
MUSIC: Israeli melody.

SHALOM
Irregular

Translation copyright © 1982 by Roger N. Deschner. Used by permission.

954
'Twas in the Moon of Wintertime

May be sung unaccompanied or with light percussion.

1. 'Twas in the moon of win-ter-time, when all the birds had fled, That might-y Git-chi Man-i-tou sent an-gel choirs in-stead; Be-fore their light the stars grew dim, and won-dering hun-ters heard the hymn: Je-sus your King is born, Je-sus is born, *in ex-cel-sis glo-ri-a.*

2. With-in a lodge of bro-ken bark the ten-der Babe was found, A rag-ged robe of rab-bit skin en-wrapped his beau-ty round; But as the hun-ter braves drew nigh, the an-gel-song rang loud and high: Je-sus your King is born, Je-sus is born, *in ex-cel-sis glo-ri-a.*

3. The ear-liest moon of win-ter-time is not so round and fair As was the ring of glo-ry on the help-less in-fant there. The chiefs from far be-fore him knelt with gifts of fox and bea-ver-pelt. Je-sus your King is born, Je-sus is born, *in ex-cel-sis glo-ri-a.*

4. O chil-dren of the for-est free, O sons of Man-i-tou, The Ho-ly Child of earth and heaven is born to-day for you. Come kneel be-fore the rad-iant Boy, who brings you beau-ty, peace, and joy. Je-sus your King is born, Je-sus is born, *in ex-cel-sis glo-ri-a.*

WORDS: Jean de Brebeuf, c. 1643; trans. Jesse Edgar Middleton. 1926 ; Luke 2:9-11
MUSIC: Canadian Tune (orig. French); arr. by H. Barrie Cabena, 1971

JESOUS AHATONHIA
Irregular

Translation used by permission of the Frederick Harris Music Co., Ltd.

1. To-day I live, but once shall come my death; one day shall still my
2. How I shall die, or when, I do not know, nor where, for end-less
3. When earth-ly life shall close, as close it must, let Je-sus be my
4. Mean-while I live and move and I am glad, en-joy this life and

laugh-ter and my cry-ing, bring to a halt my heart-beat
is the world's ho-ri-zon; but save me, Lord, from thoughts that
broth-er and my mer-it. Let me with-out re-gret re-
all its in-ter-weav-ing: each giv-en day, as I take

and my breath: Lord, give me faith for liv-ing and for dy-ing.
lay me low, from mor-bid fears that freeze my power of rea-son.
call the past, then, Lord, in-to your hands com-mit my spir-it.
up the thread, let love sug-gest my mode, my mood of liv-ing.

WORDS: Fred Kaan, 1975; Romans 8:38-39
MUSIC: Jane Marshall, 1980

HEARTBEAT
10 11. 10 11.

956
Spirit of the Living God

Spir - it of the liv - ing God, fall a - fresh on me; Spir - it of the

liv - ing God, fall a - fresh on me. Melt me, mold me, fill me,

use me. Spir - it of the liv - ing God, fall a - fresh on me.

WORDS and MUSIC: Daniel Iverson, 1926
Copyright 1935, 1963. Moody Press. Moody Bible Institute of Chicago. Used by permission.

957
Take Our Bread

Moderately

C   Refrain   Am   F   Dm

Take our bread, we ask you, take our hearts, we love you, take our

WORDS and MUSIC: Joseph Wise, 1967

958
Thank You, Lord, for Water, Soil, and Air

1. Thank you, Lord, for wa - ter, soil, and air —
2. Thank you, Lord, for min - er - als and ores—
3. Thank you, Lord, for price-less en - er - gy
4. Thank you, Lord, for weav-ing na - ture's life
5. Thank you, Lord, for mak-ing plan - et earth

large gifts sup-port - ing ev - ery - thing that lives. For-
the ba - sis of all build - ing, wealth, and speed. For-
stored in each at - om, gath - ered from the sun. For-
in - to a seam - less robe, a frag - ile whole. For-
a home for us and a - ges yet un - born. For —

WORDS: Brian A. Wren, 1974; Psalm 104:30
MUSIC: Erik Routley, 1977

ALTHORP
9 10. 10 9

give   our spoil-ing and a-buse of   them.   Help   us re-new the
give   our reck-less plun-der-ing and   waste.   Help   us re-new the
give   our greed and care-less-ness of   power.   Help   us re-new the
give   our haste that tam-pers un - a - wares.   Help   us re-new the
Help us to share, con-sid - er, save, and store.   Come and re-new the

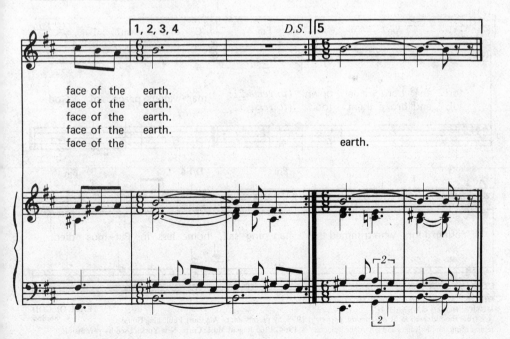

1, 2, 3, 4   *D.S.* **5**

face of the   earth.
face of the   earth.
face of the   earth.
face of the   earth.
face of the   earth.

959
They Cast Their Nets

1. They cast their nets in Gal - i - lee, just off the hills of brown; Such
2. Con - tent - ed, peace - ful fish - er - men, be - fore they ev - er knew The
4. The peace of God, it is no peace, but strife closed in the sod. Yet

hap - py, sim - ple fish - er - folk, be - fore the Lord came down, be -
peace of God that filled their hearts brim - ful, and broke them too, brim -
let us pray for but one thing: the mar - velous peace of God, the

fore the Lord came down. *(to verse 2)*   mar - velous peace of God.
ful, and broke them too. *(to verse 3)*

3. Young John, who trimmed the flap - ping sail, home - less in Pat - mos died.

WORDS: William A. Percy, 1964; Matthew 4:18-19
MUSIC: Herbert G. Draesel, Jr.,
Arr. from the *Lutheran Book of Worship*, copyright 1978, by permission of Augsburg Publishing House
representing the publishers and copyright holders. © 1964, 1965 Regent Music Corp., New York. Used by permission.

PEACE OF GOD
86.866.

Pe - ter, who hauled the teem - ing net, head down was cru - ci - fied,

head down was cru - ci - fied.

960
The Lone, Wild Bird

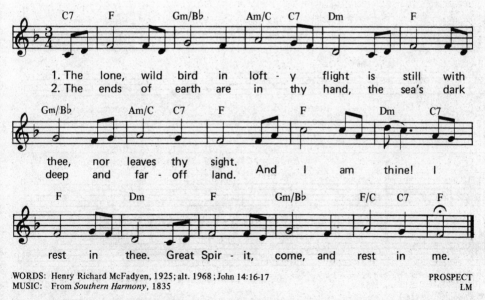

1. The lone, wild bird in loft - y flight is still with
2. The ends of earth are in thy hand, the sea's dark

thee, nor leaves thy sight.
deep and far - off land. And I am thine! I

rest in thee. Great Spir - it, come, and rest in me.

WORDS: Henry Richard McFadyen, 1925; alt. 1968; John 14:16-17
MUSIC: From *Southern Harmony*, 1835

PROSPECT
LM

961
The Lord Is
My Shepherd

Antiphon

♩ = o of psalm My shep-herd is the Lord, noth-ing in-deed shall I want.

1. —————————— The Lord is my shepherd;
2. He guides me a - long the right path;
3. You have pre - pared a banquet for me
4. Surely goodness and kindness shall follow me
5. To the Father and Son give glory,

there is nothing I shall want.
he is true to his name.
in the sight of my foes.
all the days of my life.
give glory to the Spirit.

WORDS: Psalm 22(23), Grail Version, 1959
MUSIC: Joseph Gelineau, 1953

GELINEAU
Irregular

Fresh   and   green are the   pastures
If I should walk in the   valley   of   darkness,
My   head you have a - nointed with   oil;
In the Lord's   own   house shall I   dwell
To God who is,   who   was, and who   will be

where he   gives   me   re -   pose.   Near   restful
no   evil   would I   fear.   You are there with your

waters   he leads me,   to re - vive my droop-ing   spir -   it.
crook and your staff;   with   these you give me   com -   fort.
my   cup   is   o - ver - flow - ing.
for - ev -   er   and   ev -   er.
for - ev -   er   and   ev -   er.

962
This Joyful Eastertide

♩=72

1. This joy-ful Eas-ter-tide, a-way with sin and sor - row!
2. Death's flood has lost his chill, since Je - sus crossed the riv - er:

My love, the Cru - ci - fied, has sprung to life this mor - row.
Lov - er of souls, from ill my pass - ing soul de - liv - er.

Had Christ, who once was slain, not burst his three-day pris - on,

Our faith had been in vain, but now has Christ a - ris - en, a-

WORDS: George R. Woodward ; Mark 16:6
MUSIC: Dutch, 17th cent.; setting by Alice Parker, 1969.
Words from the *Cowley Carol Book*. Copyright A.R. Mowbray and Co., Ltd. Used by permission.
Harmony by permission of Alice Parker.

VRUECHTEN
Irregular

ris - en, a - ris - en, a - ris - - - en!

963
The King of Glory Comes

Em

The King of glo - ry comes, the na - tion re - joic - es.

Fine

O - pen the gates be - fore him, lift up your voic - es.

G

1. Who is the King of glo - ry; how shall we call him?
2. In all of Gal - i - lee, in cit - y or vil - lage,
3. Sing then of Da - vid's Son, our Sav - ior and broth - er;
4. He gave his life for us, the pledge of sal - va - tion,
5. He con - quered sin and death; he tru - ly has ris - en.

He is Em - man - u - el, the prom - ised of a - ges.
He goes a - mong his peo - ple cur - ing their ill - ness.
In all of Gal - i - lee was nev - er an - oth - er.
He took up - on him - self the sins of the na - tion.
And he will share with us his heav - en - ly vi - sion.

WORDS: W. F. Jabusch, 1967; Psalm 24:7-10
MUSIC: Trad. Israeli Folk Tune

PROMISED ONE
12 12. 12 12.

964
This Land of Beauty Has Been Given

Not fast

Fm   Bbm

1. This land of beau - ty has been giv - en   by God our Fa - ther,
2. The self - ish peo - ple and not mind - ful,   the few, will claim the
3. The farm - er longs for whole-some liv - ing,   with food to eat and
4. Poor farm-ers have a right to this land,   pos - ses - sion ac - cents

C7

full of mer - cy.   Its love - li - ness has been in - tend - ed   for
land to own,   de - prive the man - y, poor, and need - y,   who
e - nough cloth - ing,   a bet - ter house, to live in com - fort   with
their well - be - ing,   for here are hopes for bright - er   fu - tures,   a

Fm   C7   Fm

ev - ery one and all the peo - ple, and each one claims his right - ful
live in want and al - ways suf - fer. And when this hap - pens there's sure
things to use in - side the dwell - ing, his child to have a bright to -
bet - ter life re - ward for striv - ing, and to the wealth - y, we im -

F7   Bbm

por - tion, a piece of land he'll proud - ly own. This her - i - tage so
con - flict, for hate and bit - ter - ness pre - vail. Re - la - tion-ships will
mor - row when he can pro - vide ed - u - ca - tion; pa - ren - tal hap - pi -
plore you, vast por - tions of your land to share. The poor have more need

WORDS and MUSIC: Elena G. Maquiso ; Matthew 5:5

PHILIPPINES
Irregular

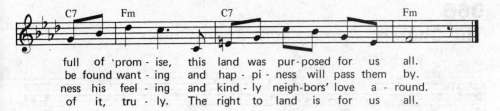

full of 'prom - ise, this land was pur - posed for us all.
be found want - ing and hap - pi - ness will pass them by.
ness his feel - ing and kind - ly neigh - bors' love a - round.
of it, tru - ly. The right to land is for us all.

965
This Is the Spirit's Entry Now

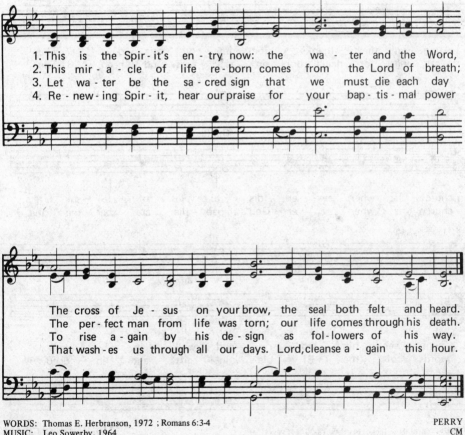

1. This is the Spir - it's en - try now: the wa - ter and the Word,
2. This mir - a - cle of life re - born comes from the Lord of breath;
3. Let wa - ter be the sa - cred sign that we must die each day
4. Re - new - ing Spir - it, hear our praise for your bap - tis - mal power

The cross of Je - sus on your brow, the seal both felt and heard.
The per - fect man from life was torn; our life comes through his death.
To rise a - gain by his de - sign as fol - lowers of his way.
That wash - es us through all our days. Lord, cleanse a - gain this hour.

WORDS: Thomas E. Herbranson, 1972 ; Romans 6:3-4
MUSIC: Leo Sowerby, 1964

PERRY
CM

966
The Church

1. The church is wher-ev-er God's peo-ple are prais-ing,
2. The church is wher-ev-er God's peo-ple are help-ing,

sing-ing their thanks for joy on this day. The
car-ing for neigh-bors in sick-ness and need. The

church is wher-ev-er dis-ci-ples of Je-sus re-
church is wher-ev-er God's peo-ple are shar-ing the

mem-ber his sto-ry and walk in his way.
words of the Bi-ble in gift and in deed.

WORDS: Carol Rose Ikeler ; Matthew 18:20
MUSIC: Trad. Cornish Melody, arr. by Jane Marshall, 1980

OLD CORNISH CAROL
Irregular

OLD CORNISH CAROL
ALTERNATE INSTRUMENTAL ACCOMPANIMENT

Soprano Instrument

Organ ped., low bells, Orff, etc.

* Finger Cymbal

967
The Love of God

WORDS: Anders Frostenson ; trans. by Fred Kaan, 1972 ; John 8:36
MUSIC: Lars Ake Lundberg

GUDS KARLEK
11 10. 11 10.

wind, and an e-ter-nal home.

968

Thou Art Worthy

Thou art wor-thy, thou art wor-thy, thou art wor-thy, O Lord;

Thou art wor-thy to re-ceive glo-ry, glo-ry and hon-or and power:

for thou hast cre-a-ted, hast all things cre-a-ted,

for thou hast cre-a-ted all things, and for thy

plea-sure they are cre-a-ted: thou art wor-thy, O Lord.

WORDS: Revelation 4:11
MUSIC: Pauline M. Mills, 1963

WORTHY
Irregular

When in Our Music God Is Glorified

1. When in our mu - sic God is glo - ri - fied, and ad - o -
2. How of - ten, mak - ing mu - sic, we have found a new di -
3. So has the Church in lit - ur - gy and song, in faith and
4. And did not Je - sus sing a psalm that night when ut - most
5. Let ev - ery in - stru - ment be tuned for praise! Let all re -

ra - tion leaves no room for pride, it is as though the whole cre -
men - sion in the world of sound, as wor - ship moved us to a
love, through cen - tu - ries of wrong, borne wit - ness to the truth in
e - vil strove a - gainst the Light? Then let us sing, for whom he
joice who have a voice to raise! And may God give us faith to

a - tion cried
more pro - found
ev - ery tongue, Al - le - lu - ia! Al - le - lu - ia!
won the fight,
sing al - ways

WORDS: F. Pratt Green, 1971; Mark 14:26
MUSIC: C. V. Stanford, 1904
Words by permission of Oxford University Press.

ENGELBERG
10. 10. 10. 4 with Alleluia

970
What Gift Can We Bring

1. What gift can we bring, what pres - ent, what to - ken?
2. Give thanks for the Past, for those who had vi - sion,
3. Give thanks for To - mor - row, full of sur - pris - es,
4. This gift we now bring, this pres - ent, this to - ken,

what words can con - vey it — the joy of this day?
who plant - ed and wa - tered so dreams could come true.
for know - ing what - ev - er To - mor - row may bring,
these words can con - vey it — the joy of this day!

When grate - ful we come, re - mem - ber - ing, re - joic - ing,
Give thanks for the Now, for stud - y, for wor - ship,
God gives us his Word that al - ways, for - ev - er,
When grate - ful we come, re - mem - ber - ing, re - joic - ing,

WORDS and MUSIC: Jane Marshall, 1980

ANNIVERSARY SONG
11 11. 11 11.

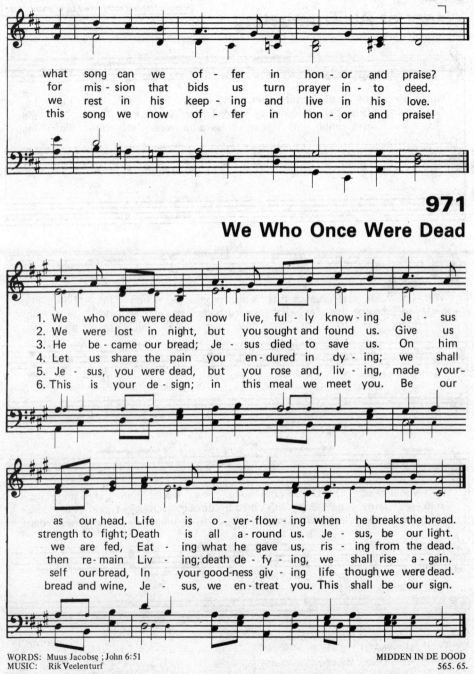

what song can we of - fer in hon - or and praise?
for mis - sion that bids us turn prayer in - to deed.
we rest in his keep - ing and live in his love.
this song we now of - fer in hon - or and praise!

971
We Who Once Were Dead

1. We who once were dead now live, ful - ly know - ing Je - sus
2. We were lost in night, but you sought and found us. Give us
3. He be - came our bread; Je - sus died to save us. On him
4. Let us share the pain you en - dured in dy - ing; we shall
5. Je - sus, you were dead, but you rose and, liv - ing, made your-
6. This is your de - sign; in this meal we meet you. Be our

as our head. Life is o - ver - flow - ing when he breaks the bread.
strength to fight; Death is all a - round us. Je - sus, be our light.
we are fed, Eat - ing what he gave us, ris - ing from the dead.
then re - main Liv - ing; death de - fy - ing, we shall rise a - gain.
self our bread, In your good - ness giv - ing life though we were dead.
bread and wine, Je - sus, we en - treat you. This shall be our sign.

WORDS: Muus Jacobse ; John 6:51
MUSIC: Rik Veelenturf

MIDDEN IN DE DOOD
565. 65.

972
Weary of All Trumpeting

The melody of this hymn can be effectively introduced and reinforced by a trumpet.

March - like

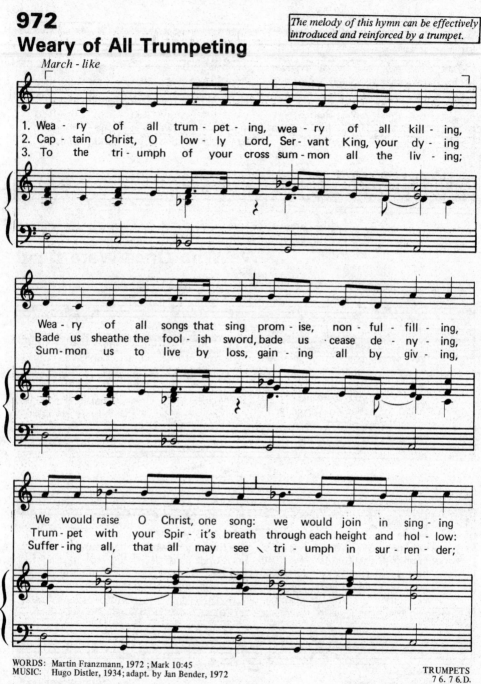

1. Wea - ry of all trum - pet - ing, wea - ry of all kill - ing,
2. Cap - tain Christ, O low - ly Lord, Ser - vant King, your dy - ing
3. To the tri - umph of your cross sum - mon all the liv - ing;

Wea - ry of all songs that sing prom - ise, non - ful - fill - ing,
Bade us sheathe the fool - ish sword, bade us cease de - ny - ing,
Sum - mon us to live by loss, gain - ing all by giv - ing,

We would raise O Christ, one song: we would join in sing - ing
Trum - pet with your Spir - it's breath through each height and hol - low:
Suffer - ing all, that all may see tri - umph in sur - ren - der;

WORDS: Martin Franzmann, 1972 ; Mark 10:45
MUSIC: Hugo Distler, 1934; adapt. by Jan Bender, 1972

TRUMPETS
7 6. 7 6. D.

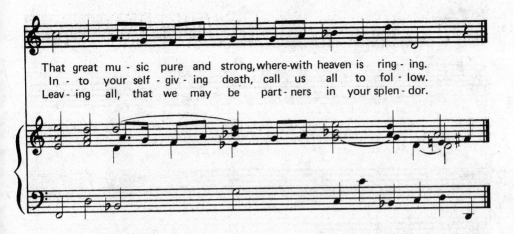

That great mu - sic pure and strong, where-with heaven is ring - ing.
In - to your self - giv - ing death, call us all to fol - low.
Leav - ing all, that we may be part - ners in your splen - dor.

973
Where Science Serves

1. Where sci - ence serves and art in - spires a strug - gling hu - man-kind,
2. Where joys are shared and fears that once lay hid in lives a - part,
3. Where mind and heart to - geth - er trust the One who makes life whole,
4. O God, bring far ho - ri - zons near, com - plete the search be - gun,

There truth and beau - ty point to God's ho - ri - zons of the mind.
There love un - locks the doors on God's ho - ri - zons of the heart.
There faith re - veals in splen - dor God's ho - ri - zons of the soul.
So what we see and dream, and what we do, by grace, are one.

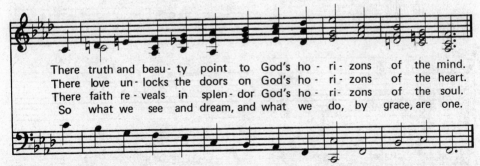

WORDS: Jane Marshall, 1976
MUSIC: Philip E. Baker, 1976

HIGHLAND PARK
CM

974
We Know That Christ Is Raised

In unison, with great breadth

1. We know that Christ is raised and dies no more.
2. We share by wa-ter in his sav-ing death.
3. The Fa-ther's splen-dor clothes the Son with life.
4. A new cre-a-tion comes to life and grows

Em-braced by death, he broke its fear-ful hold, And our de-
Re-born, we share with him an Eas-ter life As liv-ing
The Spir-it's fis-sion shakes the Church of God. Bap-tized, we
As Christ's new bod-y takes on flesh and blood. The u-ni-

1., 2., 3.

spair he turned to blaz-ing joy. Hal - le - lu - jah!
mem-bers of our Sav-ior Christ. Hal - le - lu - jah!
live with God the Three in One. Hal - le - lu - jah!
verse re-stored and

4.

(4.) whole will sing: Hal - le - lu - jah!

WORDS: John B. Geyer, 1969; Romans 6:4, 9
MUSIC: Charles V. Stanford, 1904
Words used by permission of John B. Geyer.

ENGELBERG
10. 10. 10. 4.

975

We Are One in the Spirit

Capo: 1st; Play: Em

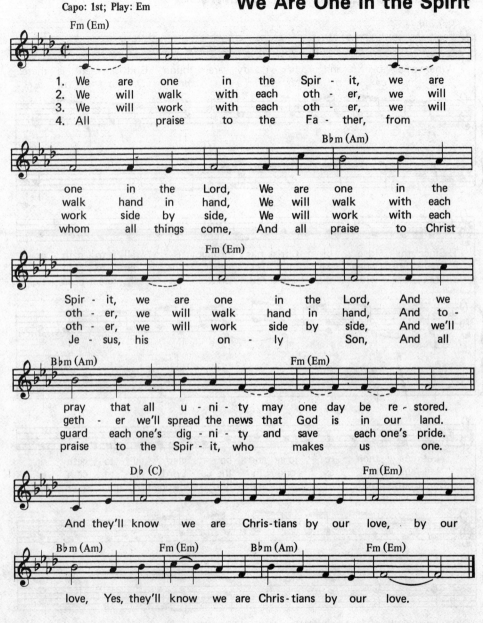

WORDS and MUSIC: Peter Scholtes, 1966 ; John 17:22-23
Copyright ©1966 by F.E.L. Publications, Ltd., Los Angeles, Calif. Used by permission.

ONE IN THE SPIRIT
76. 76. 86. with Refrain

976
Where True Love and Charity

Refrain

Where true love and char-i-ty are found, God him-self is there.
U - bi cá - ri - tas et a - mor De - us i - bi est.

1. Since the love of Christ has brought us all to-geth-er,
2. There-fore, when we gath-er as one, all to-geth-er,
3. Let us with the bless-ed ones see thy great beau-ty,

Let us then re-joice and be glad, all to-geth-er,
Let us be as one in the Lord, all to-geth-er,
Christ, our God, e-ter-nal-ly throned in great splen-dor,

WORDS: Latin Office Hymn; trans. by Richard Proulx, 1975 ; I John 4:16
MUSIC: Chant, Mode VI; harm. by Jan Kern, 1975

UBI CARITAS
84. 84. with refrain

Let ev - ery - one fear and love God all to - geth - er,
May care - less thought, ac - tion, or deed not di - vide us;
There to pos - sess joy with - out end, all to - geth - er,

And let us love one an - oth - er with sin - cere hearts.
Let Christ, our God, dwell a - mong us, in ev - ery heart.
For in - fi - nite a - ges of a - ges, for ev - er - more.

977
When Jesus Wept

Round

1 When Je - sus wept, the fall - ing tear in mer - cy flowed be - yond all bound;

3 When Je - sus groaned, a trem - bling fear seized all the guilt - y world a - round.

WORDS: Attr. to William Billings, *The New England Psalm Singer*, 1770
MUSIC: William Billings

JESUS WEPT
LM

978

Who Is He in Yonder Stall

One of the best-loved hymns of the Evangelical United Brethren. It may be sung in parts, with some of the stanzas unaccompanied.

Not fast

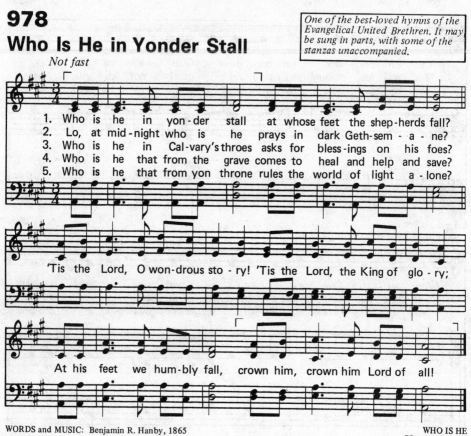

1. Who is he in yon-der stall at whose feet the shep-herds fall?
2. Lo, at mid-night who is he prays in dark Geth-sem-a-ne?
3. Who is he in Cal-vary's throes asks for bless-ings on his foes?
4. Who is he that from the grave comes to heal and help and save?
5. Who is he that from yon throne rules the world of light a-lone?

'Tis the Lord, O won-drous sto-ry! 'Tis the Lord, the King of glo-ry;

At his feet we hum-bly fall, crown him, crown him Lord of all!

WORDS and MUSIC: Benjamin R. Hanby, 1865

WHO IS HE
77. with Refrain

979

When I Needed a Neighbor

1. When I need-ed a neigh-bor, were you there, were you there?
2. I was hun-gry and thirst-y, were you there, were you there?
3. I was cold, I was nak-ed, were you there, were you there?
4. When I need-ed a shel-ter, were you there, were you there?
5. When I need-ed a heal-er, were you there, were you there?
6. When they put me in pris-on, were you there, were you there?
7. Wher-ev-er you trav-el, I'll be there, I'll be there,

WORDS: Sydney Carter, 1965; Matthew 25:37-40
MUSIC: Sydney Carter, 1965
Used by permission of Galaxy Music Corporation.

NEIGHBOR
13 10. with refrain

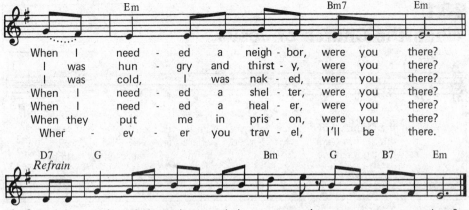

When I need - ed a neigh - bor, were you there?
I was hun - gry and thirst - y, were you there?
I was cold, I was nak - ed, were you there?
When I need - ed a shel - ter, were you there?
When I need - ed a heal - er, were you there?
When they put me in pris - on, were you there?
Wher - ev - er you trav - el, I'll be there.

Refrain

1—6 And the creed and the col - or and the name won't mat - ter; were you there?
(last time)
And the creed and the col - or and the name won't mat - ter; I'll be there.

980
You Called Me, Father

1. You called me, Fa - ther, by my name when I had still no say,
2. You give me free - dom to be - lieve, to - day I make my choice,
3. With - in the cir - cle of the faith, as mem - ber of your cast,
4. In all the ten - sions of my life, be - tween my faith and doubt,
5. So help me in my un - be - lief, and let my life be true,

To - day you call me to con - firm the vows my par - ents made.
And to the wor - ship of the church I add my learn - ing voice.
I take my place with all the saints of fu - ture, pres - ent, past.
Let your great Spir - it give me hope, sus - tain me, lead me out.
Feet firm - ly plant - ed on the earth, my sights set high on you.

WORDS: Fred Kaan, 1979; Mark 9:24
MUSIC: *Wythe Repository of Music, Part Second*, 1813; arr. Carlton Young, 1964

MORNING SONG
86. 86.

981
When the Church of Jesus

Unison

1. When the Church of Je - sus shuts its out - er door,
2. If our hearts are lift - ed where de - vo - tion soars
3. Lest the gifts we of - fer, mon - ey, tal - ents, time,

Lest the roar of traf - fic drown the voice of prayer:
High a - bove this hun - gry, suf - fering world of ours:
Serve to salve our con - science, to our se - cret shame:

May our prayers, Lord, make us ten times more a - ware
Lest our hymns should drug us to for - get its needs,
Lord, re - prove, in - spire us by the way you give;

That the world we ban - ish is our Chris - tian care.
Forge our Chris - tian wor - ship in - to Chris - tian deeds.
Teach us, dy - ing Sav - ior, how true Chris - tians live.

WORDS: F. Pratt Green, 1969 ; James 2:14-17
MUSIC: Ralph Vaughan Williams, 1925

KING'S WESTON
65. 65.D.

Music from *Enlarged Songs of Praise*, by permission of Oxford University Press. Words by permission of Oxford University Press.

Topical Index

GOD

The Presence of God
All Who Love and Serve Your City 857
As the Bridegroom to His Chosen 861
Built on the Rock 868
By Gracious Powers 867
Cuando el Pobre (When a Poor Man) 875
God Is So Good 891
Have No Fear, Little Flock 897
Kum Ba Yah 921
My Soul Gives Glory (Magnificat) 931
The Lord Is My Shepherd 961
Where Science Serves 973
Where True Love and Charity 976

Glory of God
Glory Be to the Father (Gloria Patri) 889
God Is Working His Purpose Out 892
On Christmas Night 939
Thou Art Worthy 968
'Twas in the Moon of Wintertime 954
When in Our Music God Is Glorified 969
Who Is He in Yonder Stall? 978

Creation
All Who Believe and Are Baptized 856
Earth and All Stars 880
How Good to Offer Thanks 901
If You Have Ears 910
Morning Has Broken 929
Praise and Thanksgiving Be to God 946
Queremos Cantar (We Want to Sing) 947
This Land of Beauty Has Been Given 964
Thou Art Worthy 968
We Know That Christ Is Raised 974

Gifts of God
Father, I Stretch My Hands 884
If You Have Ears 910
I've Got Peace Like a River 908
Queremos Cantar (We Want to Sing) 947
What Gift Can We Bring? 970

RESPONSE TO GOD

Response to God—Commitment
Faith, While Trees Are Still in Blossom 885
Father, I Adore You 887
Give Me a Clean Heart 890
God Is So Good 891
If You Have Ears 910
Jesus Es Mi Rey Soberano (O Jesus, My King and My Sovereign) 916
Nothing Between 933
Seek Ye First 952
Take Our Bread 957
Where Science Serves 973

Praise and Worship
Alabaré (I Will Praise) 855
Earth and All Stars 880
Father, I Adore You 887
Have No Fear, Little Flock 897
How Good to Offer Thanks 901
Könnte Singen Ich (I Wish I Could Sing) 920
Lovely Child, Holy Child 926
Morning Has Broken 929
My Soul Gives Glory (Magnificat) 931
Queremos Cantar (We Want to Sing) 947
Rejoice in the Lord 949
Rejoice, Ye Pure in Heart 950
Weary of All Trumpeting 972
When In Our Music God Is Glorified 969

Hallelujahs
Amen 860
As Jacob with Travel 859
Become to Us the Living Bread 865
Christ, upon the Mountain Peak 869
Hail the Day That Sees Him Rise 896
I Serve a Risen Savior 907
Könnte Singen Ich (I Wish I Could Sing) 920
Lovely Child, Holy Child 926
Seek Ye First 952
We Know That Christ Is Raised 974
When in Our Music God Is Glorified 969

Thanksgivings
Demos Gracias al Señor (We Give Thanks) 877
Go in Peace (Gehe ein in Deinen, Frieden) 893
Have No Fear, Little Flock 897
How Good to Offer Thanks 901
Lord, We Praise You 925
Queremos Cantar (We Want to Sing) 947
What Gift Can We Bring? 970

Hosannas
Könnte Singen Ich (I Wish I Could Sing) 920
Hosana (Mantles and Branches) 900
Rejoice, Ye Pure in Heart 950

Prayer
DAW-KEE, AIM DAW-TSI (Great Spirit, Now I Pray) 876
Our Father 942

Doxologies
Glory Be to the Father (Gloria Patri) 889
Joy Dawned Again on Easter Day—stanza 5 918
My Soul Gives Glory (Magnificat)—stanza 3 931
O God, Who Dwells in Light Above—stanza 3 935
On Jordan's Banks the Baptist's Cry—stanza 5 941
The Lord Is My Shepherd 961
We Are One in the Spirit 975

Amens
Amen 860
Go in Peace (Gehe ein in Deinen, Frieden) 893
On Christmas Night 939
Our Father 942

Going Forth from Worship
For You Shall Go Out in Joy 883
Go in Peace (Gehe ein in Deinen, Frieden) 893
Go Now in Peace 894
May the Lord, Mighty God 928

O God, Who Dwells in Light Above 935
Peace I Leave You 948

JESUS CHRIST

Advent of Jesus Christ
On Jordan's Banks the Baptist's Cry 941
The King of Glory Comes 963

Christmas
Amen 860
Born in the Night 866
Cold December Flies Away 872
He Is Born (Il Est Né) 898
Lovely Child, Holy Child 926
O Love, How Deep 937
On Christmas Night 939
Once in Royal David's City 945
'Twas in the Moon of Wintertime 954
Who Is He in Yonder Stall? 978

Epiphany, Witness, and Proclamation
I Come with Joy 904
Peace I Leave You 948
Rise, Shine, You People 951

The Life and Presence of Jesus Christ
As Jacob with Travel 859
Born in the Night 866
Christ Is Alive 870
Christian People, Raise Your Song 871
Father, I Stretch My Hands 884
Hosana (Mantles and Branches) 900
I Come with Joy 904
I Danced in the Morning (Lord of the Dance) 905
I Serve a Risen Savior 907
Jesus Es Mi Rey Soberano (O Jesus, My King and My Sovereign) 916
Jesus Walked This Lonesome Valley 917
Just a Closer Walk with Thee 919
Lord, Who Throughout These Forty Days 924
Lovely Child, Holy Child 926
Nothing Between 933
O Lamb of God (Agnus Dei) 934
O Love, How Deep 937
The Lone, Wild Bird 960
When I Needed a Neighbor 979
Who Is He in Yonder Stall? 978

Palm Sunday
Hosana (Mantles and Branches) 900
The King of Glory Comes 964

Maundy Thursday—Foot Washing
Jesu, Jesu 914
Where True Love and Charity 976

Passion and Crucifixion of Jesus Christ
Amen 860
I Wonder Why 909
Lift High the Cross 922
O Love, How Deep 937
When Jesus Wept 977
Who Is He in Yonder Stall? 978

Easter—Resurrection of Jesus Christ
Amen 860
Christ Is Alive 870
Christian People, Raise Your Song 871
Cold December Flies Away 872
Every Morning Is Easter Morning 882
I Serve a Risen Savior 907
Joy Dawned Again on Easter Day 918
O Love, How Deep 937
This Joyful Eastertide 962
Who Is He in Yonder Stall? 978

Transfiguration of Jesus Christ
Christ, upon the Mountain Peak 869
O Wondrous Type! O Vision Fair 943

Ascension
Christ Is Alive 870
Hail the Day That Sees Him Rise 896
O Love, How Deep 937
Who Is He in Yonder Stall? 978

Victory of Jesus Christ
Because He Lives (God Sent His Son) 864
God Is Working His Purpose Out 892
Lift High the Cross 922
Rejoice, Ye Pure in Heart 950
Weary of All Trumpeting 972

THE HOLY SPIRIT AND THE CHURCH

Holy Spirit
Alabaré (I Will Praise) 855
DAW-KEE, AIM DAW-TSI (Great Spirit, Now I Pray) 876
Descend, O Spirit, Purging Flame 879
O Jesus Christ, to You May Hymns 936
O Love, How Deep 937
Spirit of the Living God 956
The Lone, Wild Bird 960

Pentecost
Built on the Rock 868
I Am the Church 906
Spirit of the Living God 956

The Church
Built on the Rock 868
I Am the Church 906
Praise and Thanksgiving Be to God 946
The Church 966
When the Church of Jesus 981

Unity of the Body of Christ
Become to Us the Living Bread 865
Cup of Blessing That We Share 873
Help Us Accept Each Other 899
I Come with Joy 904
In Christ There Is No East or West 911
O Welcome All 940
We Are One in the Spirit 975
We Know That Christ Is Raised 974
When I Needed a Neighbor 979
Where True Love and Charity 976

Care for the Community
Cuando el Pobre (When a Poor Man) 875
Dear Lord, for All in Pain 878
Help Us Accept Each Other 899
In Remembrance 912
Jesu, Jesu 914
Lord, Let Me Love 927
Now Let Us from This Table Rise 932
O God, Who Dwells in Light Above 935
O Jesus Christ, to You May Hymns 936
The Church 966
When I Needed a Neighbor 979

When the Church of Jesus 981

The City
All Who Love and Serve Your City 857
O Jesus Christ, to You May Hymns 936
Once in Royal David's City 945

THE CHRISTIAN LIFE
Christian Life and Death
All That Christians Have in Life 854
As We Break the Bread 862
Every Morning Is Easter Morning 882
Hush, Hush, Somebody's Callin' Mah Name 903
Just a Closer Walk with Thee 919
Today I Live 955
We Who Once Were Dead 971

Aspiration and Hope
As Jacob with Travel 859
DAW-KEE, AIM DAW-TSI (Great Spirit, Now I
Pray) 876
Father, I Stretch My Hands to Thee 884
Fill My Cup, Lord 881
Give Me a Clean Heart 890
Hush, Hush, Somebody's Callin' Mah Name 903
Seek Ye First 952

Affirmation and Truth
All That Christians Have in Life 854
Amen 860
Built on the Rock 868

Faith and Trust
As Jacob with Travel 859
By Gracious Powers 867
Faith, While Trees Are Still in Blossom 885
Great Is Thy Faithfulness 895
Have No Fear, Little Flock 897
I Shall Not Be Moved 913
My Lord Came Walking over the Sea 930
The Lone, Wild Bird 960

Guidance
Fount of Love, Our Savior God 888
From the Slave Pens of the Delta 886
Just a Closer Walk with Thee 919
The Lord Is My Shepherd 961

Liberation and Justice
All Who Love and Serve Your City 857
By the Babylonian Rivers 863
From the Slave Pens of the Delta 886
On Christmas Night 939
The Love of God 967
This Land of Beauty Has Been Given 964

Love and Grace
And Can It Be That I Should Gain 858
Come, Ye Sinners, Poor and Needy 874
Father, I Adore You 887
Fount of Love, Our Savior God 888
Help Us Accept Each Other 899
I've Got Peace Like a River 908
Lord, Let Me Love 927
Lord, We Praise You 925
Now Let Us from This Table Rise 932
O Jesus Christ, to You May Hymns 936
O Love, How Deep 937
We Are One in the Spirit 975
Where True Love and Charity 976

Mercy and Forgiveness
And Can It Be That I Should Gain 858
As Jacob with Travel 859
O Lamb of God (Agnus Dei) 934
O the Lamb 944
O the Shame That Fills My Heart 938

Lent—Confession
By the Babylonian Rivers 863
Come, Ye Sinners, Poor and Needy 874
Father, I Stretch My Hands to Thee 884
Jesus Walked This Lonesome Valley 917
Lord, Who Throughout These Forty Days 924
O the Shame That Fills My Heart 938

Salvation
And Can It Be That I Should Gain 858
By Gracious Powers 867
Come, Ye Sinners, Poor and Needy 874
Have You Got Good Religion? 902
Once in Royal David's City 945
The Love of God 967

Comfort and Healing
Dear Lord, for All in Pain 878
Help Us Accept Each Other 899

Peace and Joy
For You Shall Go Out in Joy 883
Go in Peace (Gehe ein in Deinen, Frieden) 893
Go Now in Peace 894
Joy Is Like the Rain (I Saw Raindrops) 915
I've Got Peace Like a River 908
May the Lord, Mighty God 928
O God, Who Dwells in Light Above 935
Peace I Leave You 948
Rejoice, Ye Pure in Heart 950
Shalom (Fare Well, Dear Friends) 953
They Cast Their Nets 959

SACRAMENTS
Baptism
All Who Believe and Are Baptized 856
Descend, O Spirit, Purging Flame 879
Have You Got Good Religion? 902
Lift High the Cross 922
Like Survivors of the Flood 923
Praise and Thanksgiving Be to God 946
We Know That Christ Is Raised 974

Confirmation
You Called Me, Father 980

Holy Communion
As We Break the Bread 862
Become to Us the Living Bread 865
Christian People, Raise Your Song 871
Cup of Blessing That We Share 873
Fill My Cup, Lord 881
I Come with Joy 904
In Remembrance 912
Now Let Us from This Table Rise 932
O Welcome All 940
Take Our Bread 957
We Who Once Were Dead 971

USEFUL TYPES
Scriptural Stories
As Jacob with Travel 859

Christ, upon the Mountain Peak 869
Hosana (Mantles and Branches) 900
My Lord Came Walking over the Sea 930
O the Shame That Fills My Heart 938
O Wondrous Type! O Vision Fair 943
They Cast Their Nets 959

Psalms
By the Babylonian Rivers 863
How Good to Offer Thanks 901

The Lord Is My Shepherd 961
Rounds
As We Break the Bread 862
Father, I Adore You 887
For You Shall Go Out in Joy 883
Go Now in Peace 894
O God, Who Dwells in Light Above 935
Peace I Leave You 948
Rejoice in the Lord 949

General Index

Hymn titles are indicated by boldface type; common titles by all capitals; and tune names by italics. Composers, authors, and sources are in regular roman type.

A

A PRAYER FOR LOVE 927
Abba 887
Acceptance 899
Ackley 907
Ackley, Alfred H. w & m: 907
Afro-American Hymn w & m: 911
AGNUS DEI 934
Agnus Dei 934
Ainger 866
Ainger, Arthur Campbell w: 892
Ainger, Geoffrey J. w & m: 866
Alabaré 855
Alabaré 855
Alexander, Cecil Francis w: 945
All That Christians Have in Life 854
All Who Believe and Are Baptized 856
All Who Love and Serve Your City 857
Althorp 958
Amen 860
Amen 860
American Melody m: 857
Ancient Chinese m: 888
And Can It Be That I Should Gain 858
Anniversary Song 970
Anonymous w: 859; 874 a, b, c; 918, 928, refrain 874, trans. 898, w & m: 855, 891
Antiphoner (1681) m: 946
As Jacob with Travel 859
As the Bridegroom to His Chosen 861
As We Break the Bread 862
Ave Virgo Virginum 871
Avery, Richard, and Marsh, Donald w & m: 882, 906, 909, 923

B

Baker, Philip E. m: 973
Baptized 923
Bash, Ewald w: 863
Because He Lives 864
Beck, John Ness m: 899
Become to Us the Living Bread 865
Bender, Jan m: adapt. 972
Bethlehem 926
Betty 894

Bevan, Emma Frances w: para. 861
Billings, William m: 977, w: attr. 977
Blanchard, Richard w & m: 881
Bohemian Brethren's *Kirchengesänge* (1566) m: 856
Bonhoeffer 867
Bonhoeffer, Dietrich w: 867
Book of Common Prayer w: 934
Born in the Night 866
Boynton, Charles m: arr. 876
Brenner, Scott Francis w: 879
Bridegroom 861
Broken Bread 862
Brokering, Herbert F. w: 880
Buckhannon 883
Built on the Rock 868
Bunessan 929
Burleigh, Harry T. m: adapt. 911
By Gracious Powers 867
By the Babylonian Rivers 863

C

Cabena, H. Barrie m: arr. 954
Campbell, Thomas m: arr. from, 858
Canadian Tune m: 954
Carmichael, Amy W. w: 878
Carter, Sydney w & m: 979; w: 905; m: adapt. 905
Catalonian Carol w & m: 872
Cenédius 940
Certainly, Lord 902
Chant, Mode VI m: 976
Charlestown 857
Chereponi 914
China 888
Chinese Folk Song m: 928
Chisholm, Emily w: adapt. 901
Chisholm, Thomas O. w: 895
Chislehurst 896
Christ Is Alive 870
Christ, upon the Mountain Peak 869
Christe Sanctorum 946
Christian People, Raise Your Song 871
City of God 936
Clark, Eugene m: arr. 881
Clean Heart 890

Cleveland, J. Jefferson, and Nix, Verolga m: arr. 913; lined 884; harm. 860, 903
Closer Walk 919
Coffin, Charles w: 941
Coelho, Terrye w & m: 887
Cold December Flies Away 872
Colvin, Tom w: trans. 914
Come, Ye Sinners, Poor and Needy 874; shape-note version 874 a, b, c
Congolese Spiritual m: 920
Cotterill, Thomas w: 896
Courtney, Ragan w: 912
Credo 854
Crucifer 922
Cruz, Luiza w & m: 947
Cuando el Pobre 875
Cup of Blessing That We Share 873
Cutts, Peter m: 861, 869

D

DAW-KEE, AIM DAW-TSI 876
de Brebeuf, Jean w: 954
Dear Lord, For All in Pain 878
Demos Gracias 877
Demos Gracias 877
Deo Gracias 937, 943
Descend, O Spirit, Purging Flame 879
Deschner, Roger N. w: trans. and adapt. 953
Deschner, Roger & John w: alt. 947
Detroit 924; shape-note version 924 a, b, c
Deus Tuorum Militum 932
Dexter 880
Dirksen, Richard m: 950
Distler, Hugo m: 972
Douroux, Margaret J. w & m: 890
Dove of Peace 904
Doving, Carl w: trans. 868
Draesel, Herbert G., Jr. m: 934, 959
Drury, Miriam w: 865
Dutch, 17th cent. m: 962

E

Earth and All Stars 880
Easter Hymn (BOH 439) alt. for 896
Easter Morning 882
Ebenezer 886
Eighteenth-cent. French Carol m: 898
Engelberg 969, 974
English Carol m: 860
English 15th cent. m: 937, 943
Erickson 889
Erickson, John m: 889, 942; arr. 919; harm. 859, 908; alter. instr. acc. 918
Evans, David m: harm. 929
Evans, Patty m: 862
Every Morning Is Easter Morning 882

F

Faith 885
Faith, While Trees Are Still in Blossom 885

Faithfulness 895
FARE WELL, DEAR FRIENDS 953
Farjeon, Eleanor w: 929
Father, I Adore You 887
Father, I Stretch My Hands 884
Fill My Cup 881
Fill My Cup, Lord 881
Folk Carol m: 926
For You Shall Go out in Joy 883
Fount of Love, Our Savior God 888
Frances, Esther w: arr. and trans. 877; trans. 916, 947
Franzmann, Martin w: 972
French Church Melody m: 946
From the Slave Pens of the Delta 886
Frostenson, Anders w: 885, 967

G

Gaither, Gloria w: 864, and Gaither, Wm. J. w & m: 864
Gauntlett, Henry John m: 945
GEHE EIN IN DEINEN FRIEDEN 893
Gelineau 961
Gelineau, Joseph m: 867, 961
Geyer, John B. w: 974
Ghana w & m: 914
Giesbrecht, Norman K. m: harm. 898
Give Me a Clean Heart 890
Glory Be to the Father 889
Go in Peace 893
Go Now in Peace 894
God Is So Good 891
God Is Working His Purpose Out 892
GOD SENT HIS SON 864
Good 891
Grail Version (1959) w: 961
Great Is Thy Faithfulness 895
GREAT SPIRIT, NOW I PRAY 876
Grenoble Antiphoner (1753) m: 932
Grundtvig, Nikolai F. S. w: 868
Guds Karlek 967

H

Hail the Day That Sees Him Rise 896
Hanby, Benjamin R. w & m: 978
Hart, Joseph w: 874; 874 a, b, c
Have No Fear, Little Flock 897
Have You Got Good Religion? 902
Hawhee, Howard w: trans. 872
He Is Born 898
Heartbeat 955
Hebrew w: 953
Help Us Accept Each Other 899
Herbranson, Thomas E. w: 965
Hernaman, Claudia F. w: 924; shape-note version 924 a, b, c
Highland Park 973
Hosana 900
Hosana 900
How Good to Offer Thanks 901
Hoy, J. Edward m: arr. 933

Hush 903
Hush, Hush, Somebody's Callin' Mah Name 903

I

I Am the Church 906
I Come with Joy 904
I Danced in the Morning 905
  I SAW RAINDROPS 915
I Serve a Risen Savior 907
I Shall Not Be Moved 913
  I WILL PRAISE 855
  I WISH I COULD SING 920
I Wonder Why 909
  ICET text w: 942
If You Have Ears 910
  Ikeler, Carol Rose w: 966
  Il Est Né 898
  IL EST NÉ 898
  Imayo 938
In Christ There Is No East or West 911
In Remembrance 912
  Irby 945
  Israeli Melody m: 948, 953
  Israeli Tune m: 893
I've Got Peace Like a River 908
  Iverson 956
  Iverson, Daniel w & m: 956

J

  Jabusch, W. F. w: 963
  Jacob's Vision 859
  Jacobse, Muus w: 971
  Jesous Ahatonhia 954
Jesu, Jesu 914
Jesus Es Mi Rey Soberano 916
Jesus Walked This Lonesome Valley 917
  Jesus Wept 977
  Jillson, Marjorie w: 897
  Johnson, David N. w: 926; m: 880; adapt. 926
  Joncas, Michael m: 931
  Jones, Griffith Hugh m: 879
  Joy 915
Joy Dawned Again on Easter Day 918
Joy Is Like the Rain 915
Just a Closer Walk with Thee 919

K

  Kaan, Fred w: 854, 862, 899, 910, 932, 955, 980;
    trans. 885, 967
  Kas Dziedaja 863
  Ken, Thomas w: 935
  Kern, Jan m: harm. 976
  Kettring, Donald D. m: arr. 879
  Kingdom (BOH 314) alt. for 885
  Kingo, Thomas Hansen w: 856
  King's Weston 981
  Kiowa 876
  Kiowa prayer w: 876
  Kirken den er et gammelt Hus 868
  Kitchin, George William w: 922
  Klug, Ronald A. w: 951
  Koenig, Helmut w: 893; m: adapt. 893

Koenig 893
  Koizumi, Isao m: alt. accomp. 938
Könnte singen ich 920
Kum Ba Yah 921
  Kum Ba Yah 921

L

  Lafferty, Karen m: 952
  Latin (15th cent.) w: 937
  Latin Office Hymn w: 976
  Latvian Folk Melody m: 863
  Laycock, Geoffrey m: harm. 863
  Leisentritt's *Gesangbuch (1584)* m: 871
  Lesser Doxology w: 889
  Li Pao-chen m: arr. 928
Lift High the Cross 922
Like Survivors of the Flood 923
  Lincoln 927
  Lincoln, C. Eric w: 927
  Lindeman, Ludvig M. m: 868
  Listen 910
  Little Flock 897
  Littlechief, Libby w: para. 876
  Llef 879
  Lo Desembre Congelat 872
  Lockwood, George w: trans. 875
  Lonesome Valley 917
Lord, Let Me Love 927
  LORD OF THE DANCE 905
  Lord of the Dance 905
  LORD, WE PRAISE YOU 925
Lord, Who Throughout These Forty Days 924;
    shape-note version 924 a, b, c
  Lord's Prayer 942
  Lorenz, Ellen Jane arr. and adapt. 944
  Lovelace, Austin m: arr. 895, harm. 924
Lovely Child, Holy Child 926
  Lundberg, Lars Ake m: 967

M

  McAlpine, J. A. w: 938
  McFadyen, Henry Richard w: 960
  McKee 911
  MAGNIFICAT 931
  MANTLES AND BRANCHES 900
  Manzano, Miguel m: 875
  Maquiso, Elena G. w & m: 964
  Marsh, Donald, and Avery, Richard w & m: 882,
    906, 909, 923
  Marshall, Jane w: 935, 973; m: 865, 955; arr. 914,
    966, 973; descant 935; harm. 862; w & m: 970;
    alter. accomp. 966
  Martyrdom 884
  Mary's Canticle 931
  MARY'S CHILD 866
  Matsumoto, Sogo w: 938
May the Lord, Mighty God 928
  Mendoza, Vicente w & m: 916
  Midden in de Dood 971
  Middleton, Jesse Edgar w: trans. 954
  Mills, Pauline M. w: 968
  Mi Rey Soberano 916

Mischke, Bernard w: 873
Mit Freuden Zart 856
Moe, Daniel m: 936
Morning Has Broken 929
Morning Song 980
Mueller, J. T. w: trans. 931
My Lord Came Walking over the Sea 930
My Soul Gives Glory 931

N

Nakaseko, Kaza m: arr. 938
Native American m: 876
Neale, John M. w: trans. 943
Negro Spiritual w & m: 902, 913; w: 903
Neighbor 979
Newbolt, Michael Robert w: 922
Nicholson, Sydney Hugo m: 896, 922
19th-cent. Amer. camp meeting 944
19th-cent. Shaker sources m: 905
Nix, Verolga m: arr. 913; lined 884; harm. 860, 903
Nothing Between 932
Now Let Us from This Table Rise 932
Nystedt, Knut m: 873

O

O God, Who Dwells in Light Above 935
O Jesus Christ, To You May Hymns 936
O JESUS, MY KING AND MY SOVEREIGN 916
O Lamb of God 934
O Love, How Deep 937
O the Lamb 944
O the Shame That Fills My Heart 938
O Welcome All 940
O Wondrous Type! O Vision Fair 943
O'Driscoll, T. Herbert w: 886
Old Cornish Carol 966
Olivar, J. A. w: 875
On Christmas Night 939
On Jordan's Banks the Baptist's Cry 941
Once in Royal David's City 945
One Accord 865
One in the Spirit 975
Our Father 942
Oxenham, John w: 911

P

Parker, Alice setting: 962
Peace 948
Peace I Leave You 948
Peace Like a River 908
Peace of God 959
Percy, William A. w: 959
Perry 965
Philippines 964
Piae Cantiones, 1582 m: 918, 941
Plumptre, Edward H. w: 950
Port Jervis 906
Poston, Elizabeth m: 930
Praetorius, Michael m: adapt. 941, 950
Praise and Thanksgiving Be to God 946
Pratt Green, Frederick w: 969, 981; trans. 867

Price, Frank W. w: trans. 888
Promised One 963
Prospect 960
Proulx, Richard w: trans. 976
Psalmodia Evangelica (1789) m: 870
Puer Nobis 941
Puer Nobis Nascitur 918
Purpose 892

Q

Queremos Cantar 947
Queremos Cantar un Himno a Ti, Señor 947

R

Raphael 878
Red, Buryl m: 912
Rejoice 949
Rejoice in the Lord 949
Rejoice, Ye Pure in Heart 950
Remembrance 912
Restoration 874
Resurrection 864
Rise, Shine, You People 951
Routley, Erik w: 857; m: 958
Ruiz, Ruben w & m: 900
Runyan, William M. m: 895
Rygh, George A. T. w: trans. 856

S

Sagina 858
St. Peter's Song 930
Saliers, Donald E. m: 883
Sarum (15th cent.) w: 943
Scholtes, Peter w & m: 975
Schweizer 901
Schweizer, Rolf m: 901
Seek Ye 952
Seek Ye First 952
Shalom 953
Shalom 953
Shaw, Martin m: 892
Shillingford 869
Shull 925
Skillings, Otis w & m: 925
Sleeth, Natalie w & m: 894
Smith, K. D. m: 878
Southern Harmony (1835) m: 874; shape-note
    version 874 a, b, c, 904, 895, 960
Sowerby, Leo m: 965
Spirit of the Living God 956
Stamps, Robert J. w & m: 940
Stanford, Charles Villiers m: 969, 974
Suppe, Gertrude C. w: trans. 900
Supplement to Kentucky Harmony (1820) m: 924;
    shape-note version 924 a, b, c
Sussex Carol 939
Swanston, Hamish w: 930

T

Take Our Bread 957
Take Our Bread 957

Tallis' Canon 935
Tallis, Thomas m: 935
Tauler, John w: 861
Tessier, Albert Denis m: arr. 890
Thank You, Lord, for Water, Soil, and Air 958
The Church 966
The Hymnary (1872) w: trans. 918
The King of Glory Comes 963
The Lamb 944
The Lone, Wild Bird 960
The Lord Is My Shepherd 961
The Love of God 967
The New England Psalm Singer (1770) w: 977
The Revivalist (1872) 944
The Road 875
The Whole Psalter m: 935
The Hymnal Noted, Part II, 1854 m: 937
They Cast Their Nets 959
This Joyful Eastertide 962
This Land of Beauty Has Been Given 964
This Is the Spirit's Entry Now 965
Thompson, Colin P. w: 871
Thou Art Worthy 968
Tindley 933
Tindley, Charles A. w & m: 933
Today I Live 955
Torshov 873
Traditional w: 921, 939, 948; m: 922; w & m: 919, 921
Trad. Cornish Melody m: 967
Trad. English Carol w & m: 939
Trad. Folk Hymn m: 859
Trad. Gaelic Melody m: 929
Trad. Hispanic w: 877
Trad. Israeli Folk Tune 963
Trad. Japanese Melody m: alter. tune 938
Trad. Negro Spiritual w & m: 860, 902, 913; w: 903
Trad. 19th cent. French w: 898
Trad. Spiritual w & m: 908, 917
Trumpets 972
Truro 870
'Twas in the Moon of Wintertime 954

U

Ubi Caritas 976

V

Vaughan Williams, Ralph m: 981, arr. 939
Veelenturf, Rik m: 971
Vineyard Haven 950
Vruechten 962
Vuataz, Roger m: 888

W

We Are One in the Spirit 975
WE GIVE THANKS UNTO THE LORD 877
We Know That Christ Is Raised 974
WE WANT TO SING A HYMN TO YOU, O GOD 947
We Who Once Were Dead 971
Weary of All Trumpeting 972
Webb, Benjamin w: trans. 937
Webster, Bradford w: 936
Wen-Ti 928
Wesley, Charles w: 858, 884, 896
What Gift Can We Bring? 970
WHEN A POOR MAN 875
When I Needed a Neighbor 979
When in Our Music God Is Glorified 969
When Jesus Wept 977
When the Church of Jesus 981
Where Science Serves 973
Where True Love and Charity 976
Whiteley, Frank J. w: 946
Who Is He 978
Who Is He in Yonder Stall? 978
Why 909
Wiebe, Ruby w: trans. 920; m: arr. 920
Williams, Thomas m: 870
Williams, Thomas J. m: 886
Wilson, Hugh: m: 884
Winter, Miriam Therese w & m: 915
Wise, Joseph w & m: 957
Wojtkiewiecz 951
Wood, Dale m: 951
Woodward, George R. w: 962
Worthy 968
Wren, Brian A. w: 869, 870, 904, 958
Wyeth's Repository of Sacred Music, Part Second (1813) m: 980
Wyton, Alec m: 885, 910

Y

Yang, Ernest Y. L. w: 888
Yardley, H. Francis w: 946
You Called Me, Father 980
Young, Carlton m: 854, 927; arr. 980; harm. & arr. 857, 874; shape-note versions 874 a, b, c; 924 a, b, c

Z

Zaire 920
Zaire Congolese Spiritual w & m: 920
Zimmermann, Heinz Werner m: 897
Zion 913